Accumulating Wealth by Combining Exchange Traded Funds (ETFs) and Options Income

An Alternative Investment Strategy

by

Nachman Bench Ph.D.

authorHOUSE®

AuthorHouse™
1663 Liberty Drive, Suite 200
Bloomington, IN 47403
www.authorhouse.com
Phone: 1-800-839-8640

First published by AuthorHouse   4/11/2008

ISBN: 978-1-4343-7314-4 (sc)

Library of Congress Control Number: 2008902030

Printed in the United States of America
Bloomington, Indiana

This book is printed on acid-free paper.

DEDICATION

To the blessings of my life:

My wife, Adrienne;
My children, Adam, and Sarah; and my
grandchildren, Jordan, and Daniel.

Copyright Disclaimer and Disclosures

Acknowledgements

This book could not have been completed without the material provided by the American Stock Exchange, the Chicago Board Option Exchange and a number of other Exchanges. Special thanks to Barclays Global Investors and many other Funds sponsors and other sources of information described in chapter 11 who provided me with materials and related information.

Special thanks to the following people:

The late Peter F. Drucker, a former professor of management at the Graduate School of Business at New York University was instrumental in my receiving a Ford Foundation Fellowship in management science for research on the use of quantitative tools in management. This fellowship enabled me to pursue my education for an MBA and a Ph.D. in Business Administration. This research also enabled me to gain knowledge in the use of quantitative analysis in investment decisions.

William Edwards Deming, a former professor of Statistics at the Graduate School of Business at New York University, who taught me the theory of probability which is so crucial to understanding the problems of risk management.

Adam Bench M.B.A., my son who is currently associated with Smith Barney as a Financial consultant for reviewing the manuscript and for giving me many valuable suggestions.

Sarah Bench Ph.D., my Psychologist daughter, provided valuable insight and time spent in discussing the psychology of crowds and the individuals behavior of fear and greed.

Robert Farrell, a former Vice President at Merrill Lynch in charge of market strategy And technical analysis department, exposed me to the fact that it is important to distinguish between prices of securities that trade in the open market and intrinsic private valuation of companies.

Norman Gershman, a former executive with Merrill Lynch who introduced me to market trading and to the field of money management.

Additional help was provided by Nicholas Birns.

I also must thank the Ford Foundation for granting me fellowship that enabled me to pursue my studies for the M.B.A. and the Ph.D. degrees.

Finally, I would like to acknowledge the continued support of my wife Adrienne, in completing this book.

This book is dedicated to all investors who understand (after making some mistakes) that the most important principle of investment is *Preservation of Capital.*

INTRODUCTION

How This Book Will Help You Accumulate Wealth.

Whether you are an active investor, a day trader or someone who buys or sells securities only occasionally, I hope that reading this book can give you an edge over other investors.

There are many investment alternatives and many asset classes available to investors today. You can keep it in cash or a money market fund. You can invest in fixed-income securities (bonds), short-term, intermediate-term, or long-term, Treasuries, government agencies, high grade corporate, or high yield bonds. You can buy large-cap, mid-cap, or small-cap common stocks. You can invest in commodities and precious metals Exchange traded funds. You can concentrate your investment in one or few securities, or you can diversify over many securities and many open-end closed-end or exchange traded funds. You can invest in U.S. securities or diversify globally. You may wish to take advantage of available year-end tax strategies. You may want to give a gift of securities to a child or a grandchild.

Inevitably, you will ask yourself a question: What is the best allocation of my invested assets. What should I do today to achieve my personal investment objectives. You most likely are looking to improve the rate of return on your investments, but you also want to control your risk exposure. You not only want to make money, but you want to make money and keep it.

Preservation of capital and the mitigation of risks are the most important concepts in managing investments.

Yet, you also know that if you don't take risks at all, you will miss many investment opportunities.

Is investing in sectors, index tracking, or exchange-traded funds together with the application of options income strategies appropriate for you? I hope that this book will help you in formulating an investment strategy that satisfies your needs and will help you achieve your investment objectives.

The central theme of this book is the use of Exchange Traded Funds (ETFs), Index tracking and options writing strategies as a tool to diversify your investments, to reduce portfolio volatility and to achieve an attractive rate of return.

Managing Risk is one of the most important elements in the process of accumulating wealth. Options can be used as a tool to control risk. The tremendous increase in the popularity of index investing by individual investors, institutions and money manager, together with the huge number of new exchange traded funds (ETFs) and the large increase in options and derivatives trading volume have created new ways to add income, reduce volatility and improve the management of risk.

This book is not an attempt to teach you how to make a "home run" investment. Rather, it is an attempt to show you how the cumulative effect of small incremental gains can help you to "make money and keep it".

This book is written for both individual investors and professional portfolio managers who are risk- averse and are looking to invest a portion of their assets using an ETF equity income strategy to provide additional income and at the same time reduces portfolio volatility. In addition, pension funds and institutional investors who are also looking to enhance portfolio returns and lower volatility of their portfolios and who are willing to forgo some upside potential in order to improve risk-adjusted returns. Off shore funds and family offices should also find this strategy attractive.

There are today more than 8000 traditional mutual funds (Load, No-load, Closed-end, and open-end) The net return to investors is reduced by various expenses, management fees and by taxes on dividends and capital gains distributions. Many managed funds have difficulties beating their benchmarks. Exchange-traded Funds (ETFs). are more efficient and allow investors to utilize many investment strategies to help achieve their investment objectives. One of the most difficult challenges is finding the right investment strategy to fulfill your unique needs. This book will help you learn the pros and cons of using some of the most popular investment tools found in the market today: index tracking funds and exchange-traded funds (ETFs). You'll learn how sectors rotation strategies can make a substantial difference in your investment performance. You'll discover why so many professional investment advisors, institutional buyers, and sophisticated investors are choosing ETFs as their preferred investment vehicle. You will also find out if ETFs are the right investment choice for your needs. ETFs can help you to preserve your capital while making the most of timely market opportunities through instantly improving your diversification. They will enable you to execute trades during trading hours, match the performance of your portfolio with a particular index or a sector of the market. For example, when you invest in the (DIA) index tracking fund, you will match the performance of the market as measured by the Dow Jones Industrial Average. You can allocate your assets to fit your investment style — aggressive, conservative, or defensive. You can lower your portfolio costs and expenses in comparison to a regular mutual fund. You can take advantage of market declines by selling short and Improve your tax efficiency. You can trade throughout the day, as compared to open-end mutual funds that trade only once a day. You know exactly what you own because of the transparency of ETFs. Suppose you wish to invest in the market, but you are not sure which specific stock to buy. You think the market will rise. Instead of betting on a specific company (AT&T, GE, Consolidated Edison, Microsoft, or Yahoo, for example), you can bet on the stock market; namely, you can buy an index tracking fund such as the S&P 500 (SPY), the Dow Jones Industrials (DIA), or the NASDAQ 100 (QQQ). Or, suppose that you have some money to invest, but you are concerned that buying the stock of one company will increase the risk that you could lose money. You may prefer to invest in a diversified basket of small-cap companies or large-cap companies, in the U.S. domestic market or the international market, or in a specialized sector such as technology, pharmaceuticals, or banks. If you are optimistic about the outlook for drug stocks in general, then buying into the pharmaceutical index (PPH) has many advantages over buying the stock of one specific drug company. Whether you are new to the market or a seasoned investor, ETFs offer notable advantages over mutual funds and individual stock purchases.

This book is based on many years of personal experience a university professor, an investment advisor, and investment manager. I have helped investors plan their own personalized financial goals: conservative vs. aggressive, long-term vs. short-term, retirement planning or college planning. Now, I'd like to share my years of investment experience with you by telling you what I know about some of the best investment tools in the market today – exchange-traded funds and options strategies.

This book will help you determine if ETFs are the right investment strategy for your unique needs. They are a powerful, successful, and financially rewarding investment vehicle when invested in wisely. But are they the right choice for your unique investment needs? That's the purpose of this book — to inform, to bring you up-to-date, and to give you the tools you need to take control of your own financial destiny, and to make the most of your personal investing.

This book is based on more than thirty years of experience as an individual investor, as a student at New York University Graduate school of Business, as a professor at City University, as a publisher of an investment newsletter, as an investment advisor and manager for individual investors, and as a practitioner of both fundamental and technical analysis and the application of quantitative tools. I believe that the material described in this book will help you, whether you are a short-term trader or a long-term investor, to crystallize an investment approach that you are comfortable with — and will help you attain your investment goals and at the same time preserve your capital.

Learn from the past but invest in the future.
Nachman Bench Ph.D.

TABLE OF CONTENTS

CHAPTER 4. ASSET ALLOCATION HOW TO SELECT THE BEST ETF FOR YOUR NVESTMENT NEEDS.

CHAPTER 1

ABOUT THE EXCHANGE TRADED FUNDS (ETFs) REVOLUTION.

The ETFs Explosion

In the past few years, we have witnessed an explosion in the number of ETFs outstanding, in the volume of ETF's trading and in the dollar amount invested. In ETFs. There are over 500 ETFs listed and traded today and even more on the way. They include almost every sector and industry. There are ETFs for most broad based indexes, total market indexes, large- cap, mid-cap and small-cap indexes. There are many international and regional ETFs. (See list of ETFs in chapter 10).

According to the Investment Company Institute, the combined assets of U.S. Exchange Traded Funds (ETFs) reach $489 billion in July 2007. By September 2007, ETF assets exceeded 500 billion dollars invested in more than 600 ETFs. The number of ETFs continues to expand as new more complex ETFs are being issued. Some of these new funds cover a narrower segment of the market and many remain small.

Exchange-traded funds —funds that trade during the day like stocks with prices continuously updated — are a powerful and innovative new investment vehicle for investors today. On some days, ETFs are among the most heavily traded equities in the market. ETFs have great appeal to many investors of all levels of investment goals and abilities. With a relatively small investment, investors can own a portion of the stock market on a day-to-day basis and can match the performance of a particular index or sector of the market. ETFs are an efficient way for investors to use asset allocation, portfolio diversification, and intraday trading while maintaining two key principles of successful investing: minimizing risk exposure and preserving capital.

What are exchange-traded funds (ETFs)

ETFs are funds that are listed and traded on an exchange and use indexing as an investment strategy. Indexing is the weighing of a portfolio to match the performance of an index. An index in the securities market measures the price movements of groups of stocks, bonds, commodities, etc. Indexes for specific sectors of the market such as banks, pharmaceuticals and utilities measure the price movement of these sectors. Each ETF represents an investment in an underlying portfolio that seeks to track the performance of a specific index. In 1993, the S&P 500 SPDR came on the scene as the first ETF on the American Stock Exchange (AMEX). The S&P 500 SPDR Trust is a pooled investment designed to track the price and yield performance of the S&P 500 Index. Its portfolio holds all the S&P 500 index stocks. It is a broad market index. It constitutes a representative segment of the market of all publicly traded stocks.

Each index fund represents an investment in an underlying portfolio that seeks to track the performance of a specific index. A pharmaceutical index such as PPH tracks the performance of a basket of pharmaceutical companies, including Pfizer, Merck, Johnson & Johnson. There are indexes that track the performance of stocks of foreign countries, mid-sized U.S. companies, aggressive or conservative companies — you name it! A list of exchange-traded funds is presented in Chapter 10. Exchange-traded funds essentially are designed like mutual funds but trade like stocks. This is especially attractive to day traders and investors who wish to buy or sell at a specific price during the day rather than wait until the end-of-day prices. Traditional mutual funds are executed at end-of-day prices, which may be higher or lower than prices at a specific point in time during the day's trading hours.

For example, suppose you want to buy shares of each of the 500 stocks in the S&P 500. You have three ways to do this. (1) You can place 500 orders, one order for each stock. (2) You can buy shares in a traditional mutual fund that mimics the S&P 500, such as the Vanguard 500. (3) You can buy shares in an exchange-traded fund that tracks the S&P 500 index (SPY). With the exchange-traded fund, you can execute your order at any time during trading hours. You control the timing of your buy or sell order. In a traditional fund, you can place your order at noon, but the price that your order will be executed is at the end-of-day price. This end-of-day price may be substantially different from the price that you expected to pay at lunchtime. The same applies to selling shares. Prices may be significantly higher or lower at end of day than what they were during the day when you placed your order. Therefore, you may pay more for your buys and receive less for your sells than you originally expected.

The timing of execution (when your order is placed and executed) is important for both short-term traders and long-term investors. When you buy 100 shares of an ETF, you buy 100 shares of a "basket of securities". This basket of securities is fully transparent. You know exactly what you bought.

For example, you can buy the 30 stocks that make the Dow Jones Industrials Average index with one buy order. You do not need to place 30 buy orders to buy 30 stocks. ETF shares are listed and traded all day on an exchange. Many ETFs trade on the American Stock Exchange. Some trade on other exchanges such as the New York Stock Exchange (NYSEindexes.com).

Exchange-Traded Funds (ETFs) are designed like traditional mutual funds but trade like stocks. This is especially attractive to day traders and investors who wish to buy or sell at a specific price during the day rather than wait until the end-of-day prices. Traditional mutual funds are executed at end-of-day prices, which may be higher or lower than prices at a specific point in time during the day's trading hours.

The difference between ETFs and traditional open-ended funds.

ETFs are different from traditional open-ended funds. In a traditional open-ended fund (usually referred to by the public as a mutual fund), you buy shares directly from the fund and sell shares directly to the fund. If you call the fund with an order to redeem your shares, the fund has to buy the shares back from you at the N.-A.-V. . The fund may use its cash or may have to sell securities in its portfolio so they can pay you for your shares. Traditional mutual funds are not personalized to match investor needs. They are not tax efficient. Most mutual fund charge relatively high fees. They are not very transparent.   It is difficult to know what they own at any particular time.

With an ETF fund, you buy the shares through a broker in the same way that you would for a stock. Another major difference between an open-ended fund and ETF is that, in the case of an ETF, you know exactly how much you paid or received at the time of execution. When you buy or sell a traditional mutual fund, the shares are priced at their value at the end of that trading day. This is important if you wish to buy or sell immediately rather than wait until the market closes. An exchange listing creates intraday liquidity for both small and large investors.

In a traditional open-ended fund (usually referred to by the public as a mutual fund), you buy shares directly from the fund and sell shares directly to the fund. If you call the fund with an order to redeem your shares, the fund has to buy the shares back from you and has to sell stocks in their portfolio so they can pay you for your shares.

With an ETF fund, you buy the shares through a broker in the same way that you would for a stock. Another major difference between an open-ended fund and ETF is that, in the case of an

ETF, you know exactly how much you paid or received at the time of execution. When you buy or sell a traditional mutual fund, the shares are priced at their value at the end of that trading day. This is important if you wish to buy or sell immediately rather than wait until the market closes. An exchange listing creates intraday liquidity for both small and large investors.

The difference between ETFs and closed-end funds

Many people often confuse exchange-traded funds with closed-end funds. In a closed-end fund, the number of shares outstanding is fixed. A closed-end fund does not issue or redeem shares on a continuous basis. The market price of a closed-end fund can be below, equal, or above its net asset value (N.A.V). In an ETF, new shares are created or redeemed daily by a market maker or by large institutions. In a closed-end fund, the difference between N.A.V and market price could be substantial. The market price of the closed-end fund (which also offers intraday trading) could be above or below its net asset value due to market conditions. A closed-end fund may sell at a substantial premium or discount to N.A.V. In an ETF, the market price is very close to N.A.V, due to its unique creation and redemption process.

The market price of a closed-end fund could be below, equal, or above its net asset value (NAV). In an ETF, new shares are created or redeemed daily by a market maker or by large institutions. In a closed-end fund, the difference between the NAV and the market price could be substantial. The market price of the closed-end fund (which also offers intraday trading) could be above or below its net asset value due to market conditions. In an ETF, the market price is very close to NAV, due to its unique creation and redemption process.

How are ETF shares issued ?

ETFs shares are created or eliminated based on investors demand. ETF shares are issued differently from a traditional mutual fund and from regular stocks. In a regular mutual fund, you buy shares directly from the fund and sell directly to the fund. In the case of stocks, you buy the stock from another investor. (You buy stock directly from the company only in an initial public offering – IPO.) With ETFs, the fund creates new shares in big lots of 50,000 shares. The bigger institutions, large investors, and market makers are creating the new shares. ETF shares are issued when a basket of stocks is deposited into the fund. These stocks match a specific index. ETF shares are issued to the investor and trade on an exchange. You buy ETFs through a stockbroker in the same way that you would buy any stock. The fund itself avoids the tax consequences of trading the deposited securities. (See Chapter 8.) For some ETFs, the minimum number of shares that you can buy is 100. But for many other ETFs, the minimum purchase is only one share.

Some of the unique features and benefits of ETFs?

There are twenty-four key benefits to investing in exchange-traded funds: exchange listing, a single transaction portfolio, intraday trading and tracking, diversification, asset allocation, tax efficiency, selling short on a downtick, lower costs, market price near NAV, margin eligibility, convenience of execution, liquidity, transparency, consequences of other shareholders' redemptions, no bankruptcy, limit and stop-loss orders, replacement of stocks, hedging and risk management solutions, long-term performance, gifts to minors, falling in love with one company, cash-flow management, year-end tax-loss planning and strategies, and availability of many ETFs. These are explained in detail in Chapter 2.

Sectors and ETFs vs. Individual Stocks

Many investors and managers argue that the probability of being right on a sector is higher than the probability of being right on an individual stock. They also argue that the probability of being wrong and experiencing a catastrophic loss on an ETF is lower than the probability of being wrong on one stock. It is easy to rotate investments from one sector to another due to high liquidity and diversification.

Each index fund represents an investment in an underlying portfolio that seeks to track the performance of a specific index. A pharmaceutical index such as PPH tracks the performance of a basket of pharmaceutical companies, including Pfizer, Merck, Johnson & Johnson. There are indexes that track the performance of stocks of foreign countries, mid-sized U.S. companies, aggressive or conservative companies — you name it! A list of exchange-traded funds is presented in Chapter 10.

For example, suppose you want to buy shares of each of the 500 stocks in the S&P 500. You have three ways to do this. (1) You can place 500 orders, one order for each stock. (2) You can buy shares in a traditional mutual fund that mimics the S&P 500, such as the Vanguard 500. (3) You can buy shares in an exchange-traded fund that tracks the S&P 500 index (SPY). With the exchange-traded fund, you can execute your order during the day. In essence, you control the timing of your buy or sell order. In a traditional fund, you can place your order at noon, but the price that your order will be executed is at the end-of-day price. This end-of-day price may be substantially different from the price that you expected to pay at lunchtime. The same applies to selling shares. Prices may be significantly higher or lower at end of day than what they were during the day when you placed your order. Therefore, you may pay more for your buys and receive less for your sells than you originally expected.

The timing of execution (when your order is placed and executed) is important for both short-term traders and long-term investors. When you buy shares in an ETF, you buy a basket of stocks with one order. For example, you can buy the 30 stocks that make the Dow Jones Industrials Average index with one buy order. You do not need to place 30 buy orders to buy 30 stocks. ETF shares are listed and traded all day on an exchange. Many ETFs trade on the American Stock Exchange. Some trade on other exchanges such as the New York Stock Exchange (NYSE indexes.com).

Many investors and managers argue that the probability of being right on a sector is higher than the probability of being right on an individual stock. They also argue that the probability of being wrong and experiencing a catastrophic loss on an ETF is lower than the probability of being wrong on one stock. It is easy to rotate investments from one sector to another due to high liquidity and diversification.

ETFs Structures

There are several ETF legal structures and formats.

Open-end Index funds:.

Open-end Index funds ETFs are very popular. They include iShares, Select Sector SPDR, Powershares, Vanguard and WisdomTree.

Unit Investment Trusts (UITs):

They include BLDRs, Diamonds, SPDRs and Powershares QQQ Trust

Grantor trusts

They include streetTrack Gold shares, iShares Silver trust, Merrill Lynch Holders andRydex currency shares.

Exchange traded notes (ETNs)

ETNs are unsecured debt instruments. They include commodities and currencies. iPath ETNs are unsecured obligations of Barclays Bank PLC and are not secured debt

Partnerships (MLP's)

They include commodities linked products

Managed vs. Non-Managed ETFs

Recently issued ETFs are narrow in their holdings and are less diversified. In several cases they represent a sub-sector. These ETFs are basically managed and their portfolio composition is changing frequently. For example:

(FVL), First trust value line 100 ETF. (PIQ), Powershares Magniquant Port. (Dynamic intellidex index) top 200. (PIV), Powershares valueline Timeliness. (PYX), Powershares value line industry rotation. (WMW), Element linked to Morningstar Wide moat focus Total return.

CHAPTER 2

THIRTY ONE KEY ADVANTAGES TO INVESTING IN ETFs AND SEVERAL DISADVANTAGES

Exchange listing

Exchange Traded Funds (ETFs) trade on exchanges similar to regular stocks. What differentiates ETFs from conventional open-end mutual funds is that they trade on exchanges similar to regular stocks. For example, major market indexes such as (DIA), (MDY), and (SPY) trade on the American Stock Exchange. This makes it easier for investors to get current, ongoing information and to follow price and volume statistics. You can buy and sell ETFs in the same way that you buy and sell shares of stocks.

Single transaction portfolio

In a single transaction you can buy or sell a basket of stocks. You can buy or sell shares of an entire index tracking portfolio in a single execution transaction, just as you do when buying or selling shares of one stock. For example, you can buy the 30 stocks of the Dow Jones Industrials Average in one transaction. There is no need to execute 30 transactions. It enables investors to instantly increase or decrease exposure to a market sector, a specific country or any market index.

Intraday trading and tracking

You can buy, sell, or switch ETFs during trading hours. It is possible to get out or in several times during the day unlike conventional mutual funds trade only once a day at end-of-day prices. When a buy or sell order is executed, the investor knows exactly at the time of execution exactly how much they have paid. ETFs trade all day like stocks. You can sell at any time without penalty. You can take advantage of sudden changes in prices during trading hours.

Diversification

ETFs are inherently diversified by the fact that they represent a basket of securities. Investing in ETFs enables you to easily attain a high level of diversification and reduce portfolio's volatility.

Investors who have had the experience of going through bear markets, or periods of declining prices (1974, 1982, 1987, 2000-2002), know how important it is to have a diversified portfolio. Lower volatility and lower level of is critical to attaining long-term investment goals. Most investment advisers and financial planners emphasize the need for diversification in order to help preserve investors' capital.

When one buys a basket of stocks, one is not subject to the risk of a single highly improbable catastrophic loss due to a big decline in one stock. Your portfolio will rise or fall with the fluctuations of the sectors of securities you own.

It is relatively easy through investment in ETFs to attain a high level of diversification on one hand and at the same time make targeted investments. The goal of diversification is to protect your portfolio from losing substantial value in case of a large decline in one single stock, (due to company bankruptcy or a bond default). One sector ETF, one index ETF or one country ETF is subject to less volatility than stock selection. ETF selection achieves less volatility than stock selection. It helps to tame losses and hopefully will result in higher returns with lower risk. The benefit of diversification, cycles of over performance and under performance of various asset classes, is presented in Figure 2.1.

An analysis of annual returns for various asset classes performance data (1982-2000) shows that an asset class that was the best performer in one year could be the worst performer only several years later. For example, in 1983 Russell 2000 value was the best performer (up 38.64%), yet it was the worst performer in 1988 down (-6.45%). From 1995 to 1999, the S&P 500 BARRA Growth was the best performing asset class in each year, yet the S&P 500 BARRA Growth was the worst performer in 1993. From 1985 to 1987, the MSCI EAFE (International Asset Class) was the best performer, but in 2001 it was the worst performer (down -21.70%). The frequent variation in performance cycles demonstrate the long-term advantage of a strategy of diversification of asset classes.

FIGURE 2.1:

The Benefits of Diversification:

Cycles of Over performance and Underperformance of Various Asset Classes

	Best performer	(%)	Worst performer	(%)
1982	Russell 2000 value	+28.52	MSCI EAFE	-0.86
1983	Russell 2000 value	+38.64	LBIT Gvt/ Credit	+8.61
1984	LBIT Gvt/Credit	+14.38	Russell 2000 Growth	-15.83
1985	MSCI EAFE	+ 56.72	LBIT Gvt/ credit	+18.05
1986	MSCI EAFE	+ 69.94	Russell 2000 Growth	+3.58

1987	MSCI EAFE	+24. 93	Russell 2000 Growth	-10.48
1988	Russell 2000 Value	+29.47	LBIT Gvt/ Credit	+6.78
1989	S&P 500 BARRA Growth	+36.40	MSCI EAFE	+10.80
1990	LBIT Govt/Credit	+ 9.17	MSCI EAFE	-23.19
1991	Russell 2000 Growth	+51.19	MSCI EAFE	+12.49
1992	Russell 2000 Value	+29.14	MSCI EAFE	-11.85
1993	MSCI EAFE	+32.94	S&P500 BAR Growth	+1.68
1994	MSCI EAFE	+ 8.06	Russell 2000 Growth	- 2.43
1995	S&P 500 BARRA Growth	+38.13	MSCI EAFE	+11.55
1996	S&P 500 BARRA Growth	+23.96	LBIT Govt/ Credit	+ 4.06
1997	S&P 500 BARRA Growth	+36.52	MSCI EAFE	+ 2.06
1998	S&P 500 BARRA Growth	+42.16	Russell 2000 Value	- 6.45
1999	Russell 2000O Growth	+43.09	Russell 2000 Value	- 1.49
2000	Russell 2000 Value	+22.83	Russell 2000 Growth	- 22.43
2001	Fixed Income (Lehman)	+ 8.50	MSCI EAFE	-21.70

Source: Ibboston Associates, Standard & Poors, Lehman Brothers, Frank Russell, Citigroup asset management

Correlation analysis can be used as a quantitative measure of the level of diversification. You look at the correlation of the various asset classes within the portfolio. You want to make sure that your securities have different levels of correlation to the S&P 500 and or to each other. The quantitative definition of diversification should include the calculation of correlation for each ETF relative to the S&P 500 and also the calculation of beta. A further reduction in volatility is to invest in several ETFs.

Asset allocation

The purpose of asset allocation is to select a mix of investments in such a way that Fluctuations (volatility) in the portfolio's value will be reduced and the desired rate of return (performance) will be achieved. If one class of assets declines in value, another is expected to increase in value. Periodically rebalancing (reallocation) of your portfolio's assets will help control risk and potentially improve performance. You can buy under-represented sectors and sell over-represented sectors. For example, if your allocation is 70% bonds and 30% stocks, you may wish to change the allocation to 50% bonds and 50% stocks. You can do this by reducing the bond allocation by 20% (from 70% to 50%), and increase your stock allocation by 20% (from 30% to 50%)

ETFs are a powerful tool for implementing asset allocation strategies. The investor can develop a portfolio that fits their needs and helps them achieve their investment objectives. You can change the allocation as your needs change. You can adjust your allocation at any time during trading hours whenever the market is open. ETFs cover a wide range of the equity market and many of its sectors. You can allocate our investments by market capitalization (large-cap, mid-cap and small- cap), by country, by industry sector, or by investment style.

Asset allocation is not a random process. Alternatives are selected based on your expected returns and risks associated with each class of securities. It depends on your own personal needs and objectives and your risk tolerance. A good asset allocation is the allocation strategy that is right for you. A conservative investor profile of the proportion of asset allocation (subject to market expectation) may look like the following: Cash (money market) 5%, Bonds— long-term 10%, Bonds— Intermediate 25%, Bonds— Short-Term 20%, Equities Large-Cap 15%, Equities Mid-Cap 10%, Equities Small-Cap 10% and Equities International 5%. The percentage allocation and investments in sub-sectors will change with investor's comfort level of associated risks. Many investment advisors believe that asset allocation, rather than stock selection, determines long-term investment results.

Tax Efficiency

Investors in ETFs pay most of the relevant capital gains taxes at the final sale of the funds. It is an advantage since the money that would have been paid in taxes remain in the account and can be invested until the final sale of the ETF. It is more tax efficient to buy and sell ETFs than to buy and sell a conventional mutual fund. With traditional mutual funds, year-end distribution often results in a tax problem for investors. For example, suppose you purchase the XYZ traditional mutual fund on November 10 at $11 per share. Two weeks later, the fund distributes capital gains distribution of 25 cents per share to shareholder. The value of the holdings in the fund remains unchanged at $11 per share. Yet, the investment is subject to a tax liability from the distribution of 25 cents per share. In most cases, ETFs do not make capital gain distributions. For 2003 iShares announced that the year-end capital gains distributions were zero for all 84 of its exchange-traded funds – domestic equity, international equity and domestic fixed income. For 2007 iShares announced that year-end capital gains distributions were zero for 143 of iShares funds. ETFs offer potential tax efficiency since securities are sold only occasionally to adjust to additions or deletions in the composition of securities within the index. ETFs do not have to sell securities in order to meet cash redemptions. Thus, ETFs avoid making capital gains distributions due to portfolio turnover (a problem that exists with traditional mutual funds year-end distribution). ETFs may make taxable distributions but those tend to be minimal and generally less frequent than in the case of other funds. ETFs may have to sell stocks to match their indexes. They may also hold dividend-paying securities. You control your capital gains and losses by controlling the timing of your buy and sell orders.

Because ETFs are exchange-traded, shareholders buy and sell activity is outside the fund's portfolio. When you sell an ETF you do not sell redeeming shares, you are selling shares to other investors who buy these shares from you. With a traditional mutual fund, redemptions by shareholders will force fund managers to sell securities to meet cash requirements. This often results in taxable capital gains. On the other hand redemptions by shareholders results in trading among shareholders and there is no need to sell securities thus avoiding a taxable transaction. You should discuss with your accountant and tax advisor the specific tax consequences for your particular state and for your own investment situation.

Short Portfolio ETFs (Bear Market ETFs)

It is easy to get short exposure to the market. ProShares has 29 short ETFs. You do not have to worry about margin calls. It is as simple as buying a stock. These ETFs are designed to go up when markets go down. Short ETFs will lose value when their market indexes rise, and they entail certain risks, including , inverse correlation, leverage, market price variance and short sale risks, all of which may increase volatility and decrease performance. ProShares are narrowly focused investments and are not diversified. However, if you wish to react quickly to a potential market decline, it is an easy and efficient tool. (Carefully consider the investment objectives, risks, charges and expenses of Proshares before investing)

Lower cost

ETFs have an advantage of low-cost investing. This includes lower turnover costs, lower expense ratios, lower operational costs, and lower trading costs. ETFs are no-load funds that are bought like stocks. You can execute your orders through full-service, discount, or online brokerage services. Operating costs of ETFs are lower than operating costs of conventional funds. There is no expense for shareholder accounting. You are not paying management fees and sponsor fees, as one does in holding actively managed funds. Capital gains taxes are lower because of lower portfolio turnover. For investors who follow a long-term buy and hold strategy ETFs are especially attractive due to their lower expense ratios. In 2001, according to Morningstar Inc., the average expense ratio for exchange-traded funds was 0.48% compared to 0.89% for traditional stock index funds. With ETFs, because highly paid stock pickers are not needed, management fees are smaller than what money managers usually charge. An ETF portfolio requires almost no trading of its securities which helps keep taxes low. The lower expense ratios of ETF funds are displayed in the following table. There is a dramatic difference in expenses between actively managed funds, traditional index mutual funds, and index ETFs. This is important because fees and expenses reduce investors' returns. Chart: Lower Expense Ratios

Morningstar Category	Avg. Active Fund	Avg. Index Fund	iShares Fund
U.S. Taxable	1.08	0.52	0.15 iShares fixed income series
Large Blend	1.29	0.76	0.94 iShares S&P 500
Large Value	1.40	1.19	0.20 iShares Russell 1000 Value

			0.18 iShares S&P/BARRA Value
Small Blend	1.64	0.86	0.20 iShares Russell 2000
			0.20 iShares S&P 600
Mid-Cap Blend	1.51	0.88	0.20 iShares S& P 400
Foreign	1.72	0.99	0.84 iShares MSCI international series
			0.50-0.65 iShares S&P Regional
			0.35 iShares MSCI EAFE
Diversified Emerging Markets	2.13	0.53	0.84-0.99 iShares MSCI emerging markets series
Specialty-Tech	1.90	1.49	0.60 iShares DJ Tech

Source: Morningstar, BGI analysis, 6/02

Falling investment fees have been the big theme recently as firms sponsors with new ETF funds are attempting to lure investors away from established ETFs.

Long term "Buy and Hold" Investment Strategy

As you take advantage of ETFs lower costs, investing longer-term money in ETFs can over time substantially reduce investment costs in comparison to traditional managed mutual funds and Index mutual funds.

Market Price near net Asset Value

The market price of index tracking funds is almost equal to the net asset value (NAV). The price premium or the price discount during trading is minimal. In the case of closed-end funds, price premiums or discounts are larger and more prevalent and are influenced by supply and demand for shares.

Margin eligibility

ETFs can be bought on margin the same as stocks. Minimum margin requirements are 50% for purchase and 150% for short sale.

Convenience of Execution

It is difficult to buy all individual stocks of a particular index simultaneously. It is also expensive to buy each stock separately. ETFs provide the convenience of instant execution. When you buy an ETF, you place only one order.

Liquidity

ETFs are considered relatively highly liquid (easy to buy and sell). The market for ETFs is considered liquid because it can absorb large increases in volume of buy and sell orders with only minimal changes in prices. For example, the ETF (QQQ), which tracks the NASDAQ 100 and trades like a stock, is one of the most actively traded stocks in the world.

ETFs possess several sources of market liquidity. The natural market liquidity is relatively small, but there are other sources of liquidity. Natural liquidity is created when buyers meet sellers in a manner similar to common stocks. Additional liquidity is provided by the "backstop market" specialist with reasonable spreads of bid and ask prices. Additional liquidity is also provided by an authorized participant, someone who creates or redeems shares away from the floor of the exchange. The liquidity in ETFs is also dependent on the liquidity of the underlying basket of stocks.

Transparency

Many traditional mutual funds disclose their holdings on a quarterly basis. Their holdings often change during the quarter. ETFs on the other hand, report their holdings every day.In an ETF, portfolio components and investments stock holdings are always transparent, unlike non index actively managed mutual funds. Since ETF holdings are designed to match the performance of its underlying index, you always know exactly which stocks are in your ETF and you also know their weightings. Weighting refers to the number of shares of each holding in a round-lot of the ETF. With traditional mutual funds, many periodic reports to investors leave out discussions as to what is behind performance.

Shareholders' reports often don't explain what really caused the fund to overperform or underperform. By contrast, hedge funds are opaque and are least transparent. Hedge funds are funds that use hedging techniques as an investment strategy. They are tailored to wealthy investors and institutions willing to accept a higher level of risk for a potentially higher return. Hedge funds are reluctant to give information on their investment positions, and their reports to their partners disclose very little about how much risk was taken or give details as to what was behind their performance results.

Consequences of other shareholders' redemptions

ETFs limit the consequences of other shareholders' redemptions. In an actively managed portfolio, the portfolio manager has to sell shares to provide cash for shareholders' redemptions. In an ETF, shareholder redemptions do not affect the ETF's portfolio (due to the unique nature of how ETFs are created).

No risk of Bankruptcy or Takeover

When investing in ETFs, you don't have the risk facing a bankruptcy or a potential takeover as you might experience with individual stocks. ETFs keep you from being subject to heavy losses in a single stock. An ETF can not go out of business.

Limit and Stop-Loss Orders

You can place limit orders and use stop-loss orders, to give you downside protection when investing in ETFs. These are not available when investing in traditional mutual funds.

Replacement of stocks in an index

On occasion, new stocks may be added to an index to replace stocks that are dropped because they are no longer representative of that particular index. You should be aware that this does take place and review the holdings in an ETF periodically so that you are Up-to-date on any changes.

Hedging, Options strategies, and risk-management solutions

ETFs are an efficient hedging vehicle both for small investment portfolios and large institutional investors. ETFs can be borrowed and sold short (also on a downtick). Through the use of options strategies, ETFs can help create hedging and risk management solutions. Profits from short positions can offset some losses from long positions. You can short a sector, which you expect to underperform while being long in a sector that you expect will overperform. You can protect your portfolio from the effects of market declines and help you preserve your capital. Since you can buy long or sell short relatively small quantity of shares, small investors can better match their risk exposure. The ability to hedge an undiversified portfolio is especially attractive to executives and investors whose portfolios are primarily concentrated in one company.

Risk reduction is also one of the fundamental reasons to invest internationally (Global iShares by region or by sector). The objective of investing internationally is not always to enhance returns. Another example of hedging by using ETFs is to buy long a mutual fund (or if you already own a mutual fund) and sell short a similar ETF.

Using option strategies (Puts and calls) makes it easier for an institutional investor to hedge against a market decline. Many ETFs have an active market for their listed options. A long-short investment strategy is becoming more common not only with hedge funds but also with many traditional institutional investors.

Long-term performance (dividends plus capital gains)

ETFs are useful to investors who buy and hold for the long-term. As an owner of an ETF, you have all the rights related to the ownership of the underlying securities. This includes the right to receive dividends and other distributions from the underlying securities, if they are declared and paid to the trustee by an issuer of the underlying securities, net of any applicable taxes and fees such as custodial or trustee fees. Bond fund ETFs pay dividends monthly. U.S. domestic ETFs pay dividends quarterly. Global and international (by geographic) ETFs pay dividends annually. The objective of long-term performance is to earn long-term capital gains. ETFs are investment trusts with long-term life. For example, Regional Bank HOLDRS (RKH) has a final termination date of December 31, 2040. When the termination occurs, the trustee will distribute the underlying securities to owners as promptly as practical

Gifts to minors

It is very efficient to give ETFs as gifts to minors. For example, if you wish to give a gift to a child or a grandchild, it is advisable and more prudent to give shares of an ETF such as the S&P500 (SPY) or the Dow 30 Industrials (DIA), rather than shares of one stock such as IBM or GE. It is difficult to predict what may happen to one specific company so far into the future. It is therefore more prudent to give as a gift a diversified portfolio of an ETF index.

Reducing the risk of investing in an Individual Company

Investing in an ETF forces you to concentrate on the performance of a sector rather than on one stock. This will prevent you from becoming overly attached to one company, which may result in an illiquid long- term investment and long-term losses. Many investors will insist on holding and keeping one stock that they have grown accustomed to for long-term, even when they lose money. For example, AT&T used to be considered a widow's and orphan's stock because of its durability. However, in recent years, its performance has been dismal. The risk associated with price volatility (standard deviation) of one company is far higher than the risk associated with price volatility of an index or a sector. For example: On September 30, 2004 Merck announced that it will discontinue selling the drug Vioxx. Its shares (MRK) dropped 27%, yet (PPH) A Pharmaceutical Sector Fund dropped only 4%.

Investing in an ETF when you can not invest in a specific stock

When you wish to invest in a specific stock which is not listed in the U.S. you can invest in an ETF in which the stock represents a significant holding of that ETF. For example; If you want to invest in Samsung, a South Korean stock, which does not trade on U.S. exchanges as an American Depository Receipts, you can invest in a South Korean ETF (EWY).

Cash flow management (cash equitization)

ETFs' liquidity can be used to "equitize" cash. ETFs provide a parking place for cash. They help investors to put cash to work (during periods of cash inflows) to maintain short-term allocation benchmark targets until they make decisions about where to invest in equities for the long-term. Similarly, during periods of cash outflow, liquidating ETF positions will help meet redemptions. Investors have been using derivatives to gain temporary exposure to the equity market. Large denominations of many derivative products may restrict its application. ETFs can be used as a substitute to derivatives.(options)

Year-End Tax-Loss Planning and Strategies

"Nothing is certain but death and taxes", but you can use ETFs to implement year-end tax strategies. See presentation in Chapter 8 (Tax consideration). You should discuss this subject with your accountant, financial and tax advisors.

No limit on Shares Outstanding

There is no limitation on the number of shares an ETF can issue.

Availability of many ETFs

There are many more ETFs available today to satisfy narrowly focused investments (single industry or single country) than are conventional mutual funds or regular index funds. When you wish to invest in a narrow sector of the market you will be looking for a specific index that tracks and represent this segment of the market. However, there may not be any traditional open-end or closed-end funds available to meet your specific needs. ETFs have the availability (broad-based, sector, international, segment of industry) and liquidity advantage. Using ETFs you can get quick exposure to any market world wide.

Easy to trade

When trading ETFs, you can get in and out of the ETF multiple times during the day. It is relatively easy to trade in ETFs. When you wish to take a position in a sector or rebalance your portfolio, it is easy to do so by buying or selling the ETF representing that particular sector

Using a core/satellite strategy

Using this strategy a manager can maintain a "Core" non-managed investment that correlates to an ETF such as the broad market index, and at the same time can employ a "satellite" managed strategy that helps produce an alpha return.

Manager Transitions

In cases of changes in portfolio managers, during a transition period ETFs can be used temporarily by an institution to invest excess cash until a new active manager takes over.

Quick Exposure for cash equitization and a "completion" strategy

When a manager wants to quickly gain exposure to a sector of the market, investing in an ETF could enable (due to high liquidity of ETFs) commitments of large amounts of cash within a relatively short period of time. In a period of rising prices holding excess cash may result in underperformance. If you are overweight or undrerweight relative to your predetermined objective benchmark you can use ETFs as a tool to reallocate assets.

Global Investing

Investing internationally by using Global ETFs is a low cost and important way to diversify your portfolio and as a hedge against a potential decline in the value of the U.S. dollar.

Several Disadvantages to Investing in ETFs Commissions Cost:

Commissions is paid to buy and sell ETFs as you would when you buy and sell any stock. These costs could become significant especially for short term traders. For investors who invest often these cost could add up quickly and be substantial. Investors who follow a "dollar-cost averaging" strategy and invest relatively small amounts on a regular basis, may incur high commission transaction costs.

Trade Execution Near Net Asset Value. (NAV)

In thinly traded ETFs the price you pay when you buy an ETF may be above the net asset value and the price you receive when you sell an ETF may be below its net asset value. In heavily traded issues such as SPY, DIA or QQQ the prices of execution of trades is usually very near the N.A.V.

Excessive Trading

Because it is relatively easy to trade in ETFs, investors are tempted to trade excessively both on the "long" side and on the "short" side.

High concentration in sub-industry

Lately several new ETFs have been concentrating in a sub-industry. This practice reduces the level of diversification.

Changes in Portfolio Holdings

Investors may not wish to spend the time in order to keep up-to-date with current changes in portfolio holdings and changes in index composition. Some investors consider the practice of adding and subtracting securities from an index as a negative as they may have to change their asset allocation..

Read the Prospectus and Reports to Shareholders

ETFs are prospectus sold products. Read the prospectus carefully and the updated reports to shareholders. Find out what is exactly behind the name of the ETF. Review the investment objectives, fund expenses, the top ten holdings, know the downside risks and understand the tax implications.

CHAPTER 3

MANAGING and MITIGATING RISKS.

Know your risks

"Profits always take care of themselves, but losses never do"
Jesse Livermore in his book "How to Trade in Stocks" 1940;

In recent years investors have been faced with a "low risk premium" environment. This is a dangerous investment climate because It can be contended that investors do not get enough return for the risk they take. We live in a period of numerous risks. It is the managing of risks and mitigating risks that builds wealth over the long-term.

Risk may be defined as the uncertainty of the rate of return. The uncertainty in quantitative terms is the variability of the return. The objective is not to make a fortune while exposing the portfolio to high level of risk, but to generate above average income with below average risk. Performance should be achieved by incremental gains rather than just by taking high risks.

Investment in an ETF vs. an investment in one stock

On Sept. 26, 2007 (GLD) a gold metal ETF that trades on the NYSE, closed at a price of $72.00, a drop of $-0.33 or -0.46%. On the same day (GDX) a gold miners ETF that trades on the AMEX closed at a price of $43.15, a drop of $0.74 or -1.66%. (NEM) Newmont mining, one of the largest gold producers in the world, closed on the same day aat a price of $44.90 a drop of -$2.79 of -5.85%. It shows the different volatility of (GLD), (GDX) and (NEM) and the substantial reduction in risk (GLD -0.46%, GDX -1.66% and NEM -5.85%.) when you invest in an ETF vs. investing in one stock which is one of the largest holding within an ETF.

A diversified portfolio of ETFs.

The selection of a diversified mix of equity ETFs, non-equity ETFs (Commodities, fixed income or currencies ETFs for example) or stocks with low and or negative correlation will prevent some of the portfolio holdings from dropping at the same time that the market (S&P 500 for example) drops. Diversification is very important in managing and mitigating risks. Sector rotation is also part of managing portfolio diversification. The extent of the diversification is measured by calculating the statistical correlation.

Correlation of underlying securities

Correlation statistically measures the strength of the relationship between two variables (two securities) returns. Understanding the concept of correlation is critical to mitigating risk by improving portfolio diversification. The objective is to lower portfolio volatility as some assets returns are rising while other assets returns are falling. Correlation ranges from +1.0 to -1.0 stipulating that +1.0 describes a perfect positive correlation and -1.0 describes a perfect negative correlation. 0.0 equals zero correlation. When you combine two ETFs with perfect (+1.0) correlation portfolio risk is not reduced. When you combine two ETFs with zero correlation, portfolio risk may be reduced. When you combine two ETFs with perfect negative correlation(-1.0), risk can be eliminated altogether. Correlation can change over time. The MSCI EAFE (An international ETF) correlation to the S&P 500 has been steadily rising. From 1980-1989 the correlation was 0.58; From 1990 – 1999 the correlation was

0.75; From 2001-2006 the correlation was0.84 and in 2007 the correlation rose to 0.89.

Know the Beta of the underlying securities

Beta is a statistical measure of stock volatility in relation to market volatility. The S&P500 has a beta coefficient of 1. A beta below 1 indicates that the stock is more stable than the market; a beta above 1 indicates that the stock is more volatile than the market. For example, a beta of 1.2 means that when the market goes up 5%, the stock is expected to go up 6%. If the stock market is down 1%, the stock is expected to be down 1.2%. Beta is computed monthly for all common and preferred stocks. A low beta means a low volatility and a low volatility means low risk. However, a low beta also means lower upside potential. In periods of market declines it is recommended to invest in low beta securities. But in periods of market up trends high beta securities will over perform.

Options as a tool to manage risk.

Several options strategies are very risky but other options strategies are defensive. The use of options as a hedging tool on one hand and as a way to collect premium income on the other, makes option an effective tool in managing risks,.

Selling (writing) Put and Call options Selling premiums

In addition to diversification with different correlations by asset classes, by sectors, indexes and global investing, selling (short) put and call options also reduces the portfolio's volatility. During periods of market declines premiums collected from selling call options reduces losses from selling put options. During periods of rising markets profits from selling puts reduces the losses on short calls. Several ETFs options are thinly traded, therefore it is important to review the average daily volume and the number of contracts outstanding.(open interest).

Managing risk during a prolonged period of a bear market

Options can be used both to manage risks and to shift risks. You should identify the risk and know the extent to which risk is involved. To reduce the downside risk exposure during a prolonged period of a bear market, rather than writing "at the money" options, out-of-the-money" put options and "in the money" call options should be sold. This cash flow from options premiums reduces the downside risk. In addition the percentage allocation to cash and to short-term fixed income securities should be increased. Put spreads can also be used so that gains on one side of the spread reduce the losses on the other side of the spread.

A defensive strategy may include Low P/E sectors, high dividend paying sectors, writing puts with strike prices 3-4% out-of the-money and only little exposure to cyclical sectors.

Control the weight (overweight / underweight) of each sector in your Portfolio

The selection of a diversified portfolio mix of equity ETFs, fixed income ETFs, commodities, currencies or other ETFs together with securities with different beta and low or negative correlation will prevent the portfolio's holdings from all moving at the same direction at the same time and will substantially reduce the probability that the portfolio NAV will decline in value when the market (the S&P500 for example) declines.

Risk factors to consider

There are risks involved with any kind of investing, including possible loss of principal. Investing in ETFs is subject to risks similar to those involved in investing in stocks and bonds. Investment returns will fluctuate and are subject to market volatility, so that investors' securities, when redeemed or sold, may be worth or less than their original cost. Past performance is no guarantee for future result. Diversification through investing in ETFs may not protect you against market risk. However, it is realistic to assume that the downside price volatility of ETFs involves less risk than investing in only one stock or in one sector. International investments may involve risk of capital loss from unfavorable fluctuation in currency values, from differences in generally accepted accounting principles or from economic or political instability in other nations. Narrowly focused investments typically exhibit higher volatility. REIT investments, for instance are subject to changes in economic conditions, credit risk and interest fluctuations. Generally speaking, when investors purchase securities, they often look at the upside potential— that is, how much money they expect to make. Only a few investors look at the downside potential — namely, how much money they can lose. Investment risks are the degree of uncertainty in capital appreciation and income from investments in the future.

Investment results cannot be guaranteed. (ETFs are not insured by the FDIC.) There is no escaping it — every investment alternative involves some degree of risk. Prices of ETFs are affected by market and sector volatility. You may redeem your shares at prices above, equal, or below their original costs. Furthermore, past performance is no guarantee of future results. Investing in ETFs is an important tool in managing many of the risks involved.

Understanding the various risks associated with investments will help you avoid their potentially adverse financial consequences. The level of risk you may take depends on your age, personal financial situation, plans for retirement and living expenses needs. Through diversification over many securities, asset allocation, timely selection of different sectors, sensitivity to relative strength trends and using options strategies for hedging, you should be able to better control and manage the various investment risks. The following is a list of risks that investors may encounter when investing in Sectors, Asset Classes, Traditional Mutual Funds, ETFs and stocks in general. Investors in the securities markets including investments in ETFs are exposed to many risks.

Budget deficits, Trade deficits and the aggregate level of debt

The cumulative effect of continuous budget and trade deficits in the U.S. is a significant Long-term risk factor both to the bond and the stock market. It is just a matter of time before bond prices decline and interest rates rise to be followed by declines in equity prices.

The war on terrorism and uncertainty created by unrest in other parts of the world

The amount of resources spent on the war on terrorism is affecting many industries and makes it more difficult to balance budget deficits. Unrest in other parts of the world increases risks of global investing.

Asset Class Risk

The investment returns the securities in a fund's portfolio may overperform or underperform securities of other asset classes. Securities of a particular class may go through cycles of its own relative to the pattern of the overall market. An asset class which may be a top performer for two consecutive years may become a worst performer during the nest two consecutive years.

Increased Competition

Because of the nature of the American economic system, businesses are subject to many levels of competition. For example, suppose you are in the market for a new car. You have literally dozens of domestic and foreign models (manufactures by competing companies) from which to choose. In the pharmaceutical industry, a company may develop a new drug that could make a competing company's product obsolete. In the field of technology, products can become obsolete within a matter of years or months. As an investor, you should be alert to changes in leadership of various competing companies. In addition, Investor's capital has many choices to be invested in many industries and several asset classes. Employing a strategy of portfolio diversification over several industries and sectors of the market both in the U.S. and globally will help you control the risk of competition.

Corporate Earnings

Earnings per share can fluctuate considerably from quarter to quarter and year to year both for a stock and or a Fund. The price of a stock is often influenced by the outlook for the company's expected earnings per share or by the estimated average P/E for a Fund. It will also be influenced by how close actual earnings meet Wall Street expectations. Deterioration in earnings could result in a substantial decline in the price of any stock. Further more, past earnings performance is not a guarantee for future earnings results.

The price of a stock is related not only to past earnings, but also to earnings trend. The price per earning ratio (P/E) often depends on the historical rate and the volatility of earnings growth. Investment in ETFs does reduce the risk of changes in one specific corporate earnings, since a decline in the price of one stock may have only a minimal effect on the price of the index that includes that stock. Asset allocation to different sectors and diversification also reduces the risk of earnings surprise.

Economic Cycles and changes in economic outlook

Sales and earnings of cyclical industries such as automobile, chemical, building etc. will change with changes in the economic cycle. During a slowdown in economic activity, earnings of cyclical companies will decline, and so will stock prices. Investing in growth, value, or international ETFs and taking advantage of market timing strategies will help you reduce the risk of economic cycles on your portfolio.

Expenses and Fees

Investing in a traditional mutual fund involves the payment of management fees. These fees are part of a total annual expense ratio which can over the years on a cumulative basis be significant. The expense ratio of ETFs is much lower than the expense ratio in traditional mutual funds. Such expenses do not exist when you buy individual stocks. However, broker commissions must be paid when purchasing individual securities including ETFs.

Top Management

The performance of many companies is directly related to the ability of top management. Often when a top executive resigns or leaves the company to work for a competitor, the company will suffer and so will its stock. This risk is reduced when investing in Funds and in several non correlated sectors. Dishonest Management is another risk of investing in one stock. Investing in a diversified portfolio of ETFs can mitigate this risk

Doing Business in Foreign Countries

Doing business in foreign countries involves a higher level of risks than investing in U.S. domestic companies due to possible economic and political instability. The value of company's assets and earnings should be discounted (in terms of a lower justified P/E) to reflect these additional risks.

Int'l Investments, Foreign Currency Fluctuations and the Value of the dollar

Int'l investments may involve capital loss from unfavorable fluctuations in currency values, from differences in generally accepted accounting principles or from economic and political instability. Investors in ETFs with international exposure are taking additional risks due to potential unfavorable fluctuations in currency values. Foreign earnings in U.S. dollars will fluctuate with changes in the value of the dollar. This risk can be reduced by investing in Global Funds and by selecting sectors where portfolio holdings derive a large percentage of revenues from outside the U.S. This could result in an additional risk or a new opportunity. A steady decline in the value of the dollar raises the risks of inflation and increases the long term level of interest rates.

Government Regulations and Policy Errors

Several Industries are subject to intensive government regulation. For example: The Food and Drug Administration, could prevent a drug company from marketing a new drug or force a company to withdraw a drug from the market. An existing drug could be taken off the market because of new finding of health problems discovered in later years. This may cause a specific stock to drop sharply. In these cases buying the Industry ETF (For example; PPH or XLV) will substantially reduce investment risks. Government regulation and changes in government regulations of certain sectors such as Healthcare (IYH, VHT, XLV), Pharmaceuticals (PPH), Utilities (IDU, UTH, VTU, XLU), Telecommunication (IYZ, TTH) could affect the performance of any specific sector. Governments tend to pursue aggressive legislation reacting to short-term troubles like fire trucks respond to false alarms. They often over react near the top and near the bottom of free market cycles. Government protectionism is another risk facing the benefits of a global economy and international trade. The Federal Reserve may aggressively tighten creating (with a lead time) an economic slowdown.

Industry –Wide Problems

One industry may face unique problems during one period or another. For example, when the price of oil rises, all airlines are adversely affected. Similarly, when mortgage rates go up, building stocks suffer. When you buy ETFs you can invest in different industries and reduce your risk exposure associated with investing in one industry.

Inflation and commodity prices

Inflation can be defined as rising prices and costs of goods and services (food, rent, wages, etc.). In effect, for the same quantity and quality of goods and services, you have to pay more than previously. Inflation is hard on everyone, especially on retired persons and those who may have invested heavily in long-term bonds. Let's look at these two areas more closely.

Inflation adversely affects most retired people because they often must depend on fixed retirement income. As prices go up, you as a retired person may have to spend more money to maintain the same standard of living, while at the same time your income may remain unchanged. In many cases, because of improper financial planning, retired people have to reduce their standard of living. Namely, they can afford to buy fewer goods and services.

When you buy fixed income securities, such as bonds and high dividend yield stocks, you are subject to the risk of inflation. As interest rises, the value of fixed income securities declines. You can hedge against inflation by changing your asset allocation and investing in sectors such as Real Estate Investment Trust (REITS), Utilities, Energy sector, metals (Gold) and growth stocks that benefit from rising prices of goods and services. You should consider reducing your asset allocation to fixed income securities (bonds) and increase your allocation to sectors that benefit from inflation and industries that can pass along to the consumer increasing costs.

Changes in Interest Rates

The market prices of Fixed-income securities (bonds) and dividend paying stocks (utilities) directly correlate to interest rates levels. As interest rates rise, bonds decline in value. High dividend paying stocks are also sensitive to changes in interest rates. Therefore, your outlook for both short term and long term rates will have an important impact on your investment allocation to Funds. By changing the mix of relative investments in the various sectors of the market you can reduce the risk and increase the return associated with changes in interest rates.

Lawsuits and consumer claims

Many companies and several industries are subject to lawsuits by consumers and by the government. These lawsuits are often damaging to the companies involved and to its shareholders. Drug companies dealing with health-related regulations are especially vulnerable to this kind of risk. Asbestos-related lawsuits have caused several companies to declare bankruptcy. This is just another example for the need to diversify by investing in a group of ETFs.

Liquidity

When a large volume of trading results only in little change in price we know that there is enough liquidity in the options volume and in its underlying securities.. Under certain market conditions or in the case of smaller companies, you may encounter difficulty buying or selling a relatively large number of shares. If you have to sell your stock in a hurry, your investment return could suffer simply because you might be forced to sell at a lower price due to lack of liquidity. Investing in ETFs substantially reduces the risk of liquidity because of their unique process of creating additional shares as needed. Should you plan to sell covered call options against your long Funds position, or if you consider buying put options, the liquidity of listed options is critical as to the selection of your Fund.

Market Trading Risks

An ETF's net asset vale (N.A.V) will react to movements in the stock and bond markets. An investor could lose money over short periods due to fluctuations in a Fund's N.A.V in response to market movements, and over longer periods during market downtrends. The value of your investment could decline due to an overall market decline with little relationship to the fundamental business performance of a company. The business fundamentals of a company could actually be improving, yet due to market condition, the price of the stock or the Fund may fall. Therefore, the timing of buy and sell decisions is important. Most of the time during a market cycle some timing indicators will give you a bullish reading and some will give you a bearish reading. It is very unlikely that all indicators will be bullish or all indicators will be bearish at any given time. Therefore market timing risks always exist. Secondary market trading in funds shares on the AMEX, NYSE, CBOE, or other exchanges may be halted due to market conditions or for other reasons such as "circuit breaker" rules caused by extraordinary market volatility.

Over Concentration in few Investments

Several new ETFs focus on very specific small segments of the market. They lack adequate diversification as the Index they track may own only few stocks. Investors frequently concentrate their investments in one specific stock or in few specific sectors. Over concentration could involve a high degree of risk. Fortunes of companies do change over time. What may seem to be today an excellent company with a promising future could end up in bankruptcy due to competition and technological innovations just in later years. This risk can be reduced through diversification over several sectors and by monitoring and rotating from under performing to over performing sectors.

Changes in tax rates and tax treatment
of Business transactions.

You should consult your tax advisor as to recent changes in the tax laws. Questions related to the alternative minimum tax, tax rates on qualified dividends, municipal bonds, long-term and short-term capital gains, domestic and global income and laws related to options trading. When planning your investment strategies take into consideration potential future tax changes that may affect your investment allocation.

Tax laws are inevitably subject to frequent changes. As a result, the tax advantages or disadvantages of various investment strategies will also change. These changes could put you at risk of making the wrong financial decisions, including asset allocation. For example, in 2003, the U.S. government changed the tax status of corporate dividends. Whether or not a dividend is tax-free would be important in determining if you wish to invest in a sector that pays a high or above average dividends. The tax treatment of long-term capital gains may also have a significant impact on your choice of investment strategies. (You do not pay taxes on unrealized capital gains). Your accountant and or your tax advisor should help you decide if it's more advantageous for you to invest in

Tracking Errors

ETFs are supposed to follow the indexes they track. But sometimes there is a difference in the performance of the ETf and the performance of the Index it is supposed to track. The ETF will diverge more when it tracks less-liquid securities. Shares of ETFs may trade at prices slightly below or above Net Asset Value due to the Unique creation process of ETF shares, small discounts or premium to NAV may exist but for only short period of time. Large discounts or premiums should not be sustained for long period of time. Unlike shares of closed-end funds (where the number of shares outstanding is fixed) they frequently trade above or below their NAV due to changes in investor's demand. Imperfect correlation between securities in an ETF and those in its underlying index may cause the fund's returns to deviate from the return of the underlying index. Due to market liquidity, it is possible for the Dow Jones Industrial Average index to increase by 1% in a given day, but the ETF (DIA) may go up slightly more or slightly less than 1%..Companies included in the utilities HOLDRS are considered to be involved in various segments of the utilities industry, yet the price movements of the utilities HOLDRS may not necessarily follow the movements of the utilities industry in general. Distribution of cash and dividends received by the funds may be delayed when compared to direct ownership of the underlying securities. Shares of closed-end funds frequently trade at a discount from their net asset value.

Standard Deviation and the Sharpe Ratio

Standard Deviation measures the variability of returns of an investment Portfolio. It is a measure of risk. An investment with a higher standard deviation is an investment with higher risk. It is the square root of the variance. The variance is equal to the sum of the square of (each individual observation Xi) minus (average Xi) and divided by N-1. N is the number of observations.

Lower standard deviation and lower correlation add potential alpha to the portfolio. The Sharpe Ratio is a quantitative measure of risk-adjusted return. A higher Sharpe ratio Entails a higher risk-adjusted investment return and a lower Sharpe ratio entails a lower Risk adjusted return.. Risk averse investors seek to maximize the value of Sharpe ratio. It is calculated by dividing the excess return (the investment return less the risk-free return) by the investment's standard deviation. It uses standard deviation as a description of risk. The standard deviation and the Sharpe ratio are a quantitative description of risk.

A Black Swan Event

"A black swan" event is a highly improbable event with three principal characteristics: It is unpredictable; it carries a massive impact; and, after the fact, we concoct an explanation that makes it appear less random, and more predictable, than it was "The Black Swan (The impact of the highly improbable) by Nassim Nicholas Taleb.

New York: Random House 2007.

The crash of 1929 was a Black Swan event. What is the risk or the probability of having another 1929-like stock market crash? Can you protect your portfolio from a black Swan event? And what is the cost you have to pay for that protection?

To mitigate that type of a risk you can always have some investment in one of the ultra short (inverse correlation) ETFs. For example; DXD, EEV, QID, and SDS. (See chapter 10 for a complete list of Bear Market ETFs)

Summary; Risks, Uncertainty, Investment Returns and a non-directional portfolio

There is a distinction between risks and uncertainty. Risk is one where probabilities can be assigned with confidence. Uncertainty is different. There are no precise probabilities to rely on. When managing risk it is important that you understand and define the probability of Risks. The desire to achieve above-average investment returns often results in taking above-average risks. Higher returns often have meant higher volatility in investment values and higher risks which occasionally produce lower or even negative returns and loss of principal. Each investor should try to quantify his or her own risk tolerance as part of defining their investment objectives. If you consider yourself an aggressive or a conservative investor, or if your objectives are growth and or income, you must realize that seeking above average returns is often accompanied by exposing yourself to above average risks. To better evaluate the risks involved in investing in a specific Fund, a specific Sector, or a combinations of sectors, always go over the most recent prospectus. Read it carefully before you invest.

A non-directional portfolio.

To reduce the downside risk, you should make sure that your portfolio holdings do not all move in the same direction. When some holdings decline in price, other should rise in price. The portfolio beta should be reduced near market tops when prices are high and should be increased near market bottoms when prices are low.

"Common stocks should be purchased when their prices are low, not after they have risen to high levels during an upward bull market. Buy, when everyone else is selling, and hold until everyone else is buying – This is the very essence of successful investments"

J. Paul Getty

CHAPTER 4

ASSET ALLOCATION HOW TO SELECT THE BEST ETF FOR YOUR INVESTMENT NEEDS.

Allocation and Risks

The amount you allocate among your investment alternatives depends on your risk profile and your risk tolerance. For higher risk tolerance you can accept greater volatility (Higher beta securities). With lower risk profile you should accept lower volatility (Lower Beta securities or ETFs).

Asset Allocation: A Key to Portfolio Performance.

With more than 600 ETFs available, (iShares alone has more than 140 different ETFs)You have the opportunity to allocate your portfolio assets among many asset classes (growth or value, large-cap or small-cap, domestic or international, fixed income, countries or sectors See a complete list of ETFs in chapter 10). Any single ETF or a combination of ETFs from a list of over 500, is a candidate for being included in your asset allocation. The mix of assets among many available investment alternatives will, to a great degree, determine the long-term performance of the portfolio. ETFs have the advantage of instant diversification, high liquidity, and low transaction costs, which makes them an important tool for executing "sector mix" adjustments. Asset allocation is a systematic way of determining a mix of investments that will help in achieving long-term targets of rate of return (performance) subject to the investor's tolerance for risk.

Keeping all your eggs in one basket could result in one catastrophic mistake (a stock that you own declares bankruptcy). Asset allocation forces you to follow a more disciplined investment policy and implementation procedure. You learn from the past, but you invest in the future. Past performance does not guarantee future results. A 70% – 30% stocks to bonds allocation was good for the ten-year period of 1990–2000, but it may not be as successful during the next ten-year period of 2000–2010. There are always times when some sectors of the market act better than others. After experiencing a market decline (2000–2002), investors have been looking for ways to minimize the downside risk of their portfolios. ETFs are flexible tools to diversify portfolios and make changes in asset mix in order to adjust to changes in percentage allocation created by market fluctuations.

Efficient portfolio construction

Asset allocation has been around for years. There are different investment alternatives (such as money market, stocks, bonds, global securities, real estate, commodities etc.). Depending on market and economic conditions, each investment vehicle may at various times underperform or overperform. During 2007 Energy (Oil) ETFs, Latin America and China ETFs were the areas to be overweight. Investment in ETFs is a very efficient way to construct your portfolio.

Mitigating risks

You mitigate risk by reducing volatility and by the transfer of risk. Lower volatility can be achieved by carefully selecting securities with different correlation and different beta.Using options strategies can be an important tool to reduce risks.

Meet diversification goals

There is an old saying: "Don't put all your eggs in one basket." Different baskets (different ETFs) should move in different direction as the market declines. The market can be defined as the S&P 500 or the Russell 3000 for example. Try to avoid having a one-directional portfolio. You should aim at having a non-directional portfolio.

A detailed list of Exchange Traded Funds by industries, sectors, asset classes, large-cap, mid-cap. small-cap, fixed income securities and global and Regional. Commodities and currencies, is presented in Chapter 10.

Switching from one asset class to another by rotating sectors, may take place in response to changes in the level of interest rates and changes in the outlook for profits as wells as changes in the investor's needs and objectives. The overall objective of asset allocation together with sector rotation is enhancing performance and at the same time increase diversification and reduce risks associated with portfolio volatility . Suppose your long-term target allocation is 50% bonds and 50% stocks, and the 50% stocks are further allocated to 25% growth and 25% value. When interest rates drop, bond values go up. This may increase the bond value allocation of the portfolio to 60% and reduce the stock value allocation to 40%. In order to maintain the 50% / 50% long-term allocation target, you will have to sell some bonds and buy some stocks. Stocks could be further allocated not only between growth and value, but also between large-cap, mid-cap and small-cap, or between domestic and international.

Beta and correlation

When selecting ETFs, you should take into consideration the correlation to the market of each ETF. (Market can be defined as the S&P 500 or Russell 3000 for example). The selection of different correlation will assure that the portfolio is non-directional. During periods of market declines the selection of ETFs should concentrate on low Beta (low volatility) securities. During periods of rising markets the selection should include high Beta securities.

Availability of listed options

Not all ETFs have listed options. For investment strategies that involve Covered writing, selling cash covered puts, or the use of options for hedging, it is important to check that options are liquid, and that the spread between the bid and the asked is narrow. The availability of listed options may be a consideration in asset allocation decisions.

The use of Fundamental analysis in Asset Allocation

Traditional fundamental analysis that includes; dividends yields, Price per Earnings ratios, Book values and Price per book ratios, Earnings growth rates and Beta and correlation information, can be used to rank the attractiveness of each ETF.

Technical considerations in asset allocation

Trends analysis, support and resistance formations, moving averages, VIX and TRIN indicators and volume activity can be used as a tool for investment timing decisions.

Key Questions to Ask before you allocate

- When and how often should you reallocate
- What percentage allocation adjustment should you make in each sector
- Should you use short-term or long-term quantitative analysis
- Should you be a contrarian or follow the momentum
- * Is the ETF overvalued or undervalued using "fundamental" analysis
- * Is the sector temporarily out of favor creating a buy opportunity
- * What is the growth outlook for that ETF
- * What is the dividend yield
- * What is the P/E Ratio

- Are listed options available and are they actively traded
* What is the Correlation of the sector relative to the S&P 500
- What is the level of Beta

All these type of questions are an ongoing process for investors. It is also very important To understand and know the profile of each ETF.

Criteria for Selecting ETFs.

Selecting one or more ETFs should be based on investors' needs (dividend income or capital gains), objectives, and risk tolerance. The selection could be based on technical analysis such as "the trend is your friend" approach, money flow into sectors, or on fundamental analysis such as P/E, dividends and growth rates or economic cycles. For example, the P/E ratio for the S&P 500 in 1987 dropped from about 17 to 11 P/E. For the period 1998 to 2002, the P/E dropped from about 29 to about 17. Asset allocation among ETFs could be based on relative strength calculations, event driven and/or short-term and long-term outlook for any specific sector. Options strategies could be used to generate additional income (covered calls) or for portfolio hedging (puts). The allocation decision could use "group allocation decision models," as recommended by various brokerage firms. You can utilize the changes in analyst recommendations of BUY, SELL, or HOLD and reduce or increase the allocation by adjusting to upgrades or downgrades issued by analysts. Index components should also be taken into consideration when evaluating several similar sectors. Dividend yield may determine the final selection when income objectives are important. Investment in ETFs forces you to be disciplined, to plan and decide in which sectors of the market you wish to invest in order to achieve your investment objectives.

Review for possible overlap of ETF's holdings

You should examine the holdings of each ETF to see to what extent holdings overlap.For example: Compare the holdings of (XLF) the Financial Select Sector SPDR to the Holdings of (DVY) the Dow Jones Dividend Select. The Industry diversification of (DVY) shows that as of 09-30-07, 39.9% of the portfolio was invested in Financials. The (XLF) holdings were 99.9% in Financials. During October-November 2007 the (XLF) declined sharply and underperformed and because of the (DVY) exposure to financials the combination of (XLF) and (DVY) did not produce the desired diversification.

How To Match ETFs To Your Investment Objectives

Selecting the best ETFs for your portfolio—and the investment strategy most appropriate for you — depends on your unique personal situation. Answering the following questions will help you and your financial advisor manage your investments more efficiently.

1. What are your overall investment objectives?
   a. preservation of capital
   b. long-term growth
   c. income plus growth
   d. income
   e. other

2. What are your current income requirements?
   a. Taxable income
   b. Tax free income
   c. Current income not important
   d. Long-term capital gains

3. What is your age bracket?
   a. 0 - 18
   b. 18 - 35

c. 35 - 55
d. over 55

4. What is your approximate income bracket?
   a. under 50,000 annually
   b. $50,000 to $200,000
   c. $200,000 - $500,000
   d. over $500,000

5. What is your investment holding time horizon?
   a. Short-term, less than 4 years
   b. Intermediate-term 4 to 9 years
   c. Long-term, more than 9 years

6. What is your risk tolerance?
   a. Low risk, income return
   b. Moderate risk for moderate return
   c. Above-average risk for above-average return
   d. High risk for high return

7. Which size of companies do you prefer?
   a. Small-cap
   b. Mid-cap
   c. Large-cap
   d. All the above

8. What is your tolerance for volatility?
   a. Low volatility
   b. High volatility
   c. You prefer stop-loss orders

9. What is your comfort level with international investments?
   a. Allocation by country
   b. Which percentage outside U.S.?

10. What is your preferred allocation between bonds and stocks?
    a. percent in equities
    b. percent in bonds

11. Do you have any ERISA restrictions?

Dividend yields of ETFs and Asset Allocation

Historically, dividends account for about 75% of the total return of the S&P500. The S&P 500 on an average rose 7% a year, net after inflation, and about 5% out of the 7% increase came from dividends. Since dividends are such an important component of the total return for equities investments, it should be taken into consideration in asset allocation decisions. During periods of slow economic and earnings growth, and in a bear market or sideway price movements environment, allocating more assets to sectors with high dividends (such as Consumer Staples, Financials, REITS, Utilities, etc.) is recommended. Sectors generating above average cash flows that support future increase in dividends are also very attractive. Tax reduction and favorable tax treatment of dividends increases the attractiveness of investing in sectors with free cash flow which increases the ability to raise present and future dividends payout ratios.

There are four dividend dates for shareholders: Declaration date, payable date, Ex - dividend date, and record date. The declaration date is the day when an announcement is made that a dividend will be paid. Payable date is the day when the dividend is actually paid to shareholders. Ex-dividend date is the day the stock begins trading without the dividend. Record date is the day the investor owns the stock. (When you buy or sell a stock, it takes three days to settle a trade.)

The dividend policy of each ETF should be checked in the relevant prospectus. There is no guarantee that dividends will be paid. The frequency of the dividends may vary depending on the ETF. For example, global iShares ETFs pay dividends annually.

U.S. iShare ETFs pay dividends quarterly. Fixed-income iShares ETFs pay dividends monthly. DIA pays dividends monthly. If dividends are an important consideration in your selection of an ETF, you should check in the prospectus to find out how often the ETF pays dividends. Investment decisions of ETFs are often influenced by their dividend yield. An important part in determining the value and the relative attractiveness of ETFs is the payout of cash dividends and the dividend yield. (See a list of top yielding ETFs in chapter 9). For information regarding dates and amounts of distribution of dividends, check sources of information such as swww.etfconnect.com , yahoo finance or www.AMEX.com.

Many available ETFs

A detailed list of over 500 available ETFs is presented in chapter 10. To achieve a satisfactory level of diversification you probably need to select about 30 ETFs

An Example of Portfolio Asset Allocation:

The ongoing decision for asset allocation depends on whether your investment objectives are conservative, moderate conservative, moderate, moderate aggressive or aggressive. You should be committed to disciplined diversification. The selection of various sectors should be dynamic and subject to periodic rotation. The allocation should depend on you risk profile. The following are some suggestions regarding possible percentage of asset allocation.

Conservative Portfolio

As a conservative investor you should invest in stable investments with low volatility. The assumption is that you are at or near retirement age and you do not tolerate short term volatility. The recommended allocation for example may look like this:

Cash Equivalent: Money Market	20%
Bonds Fixed Income	35%
(AGG, BSV, IEI, ITE, SHV, SHY)	
Inflation Adjusted Bonds (TIP)	15%
Equities Domestic (SPY, DIA)	15^
Utilities (XLU)	5%
Equities Global (VEU)	5%
Precious Metals, Commodities	5%
(GDX, DBA)	

Moderate Portfolio

Cash Equivalent: Money Market	10%
Bonds Fixed Income	28%
(AGG, BSV, IEI, ITE, SHV, SHY)	
Inflation Adjusted bonds (TI)	10%
Equities Domestic (SPY, DIA, VTI)	30%
Large-cap Russell 1000 (IWB)	4%
REITS (IYR, RWX)	2%
Utilities (XLU)	4%
Equities Global (VEU)	9%
Precious Metals, Commod. (GDX, DBA)	3%

Aggressive Portfolio

Cash Equivalent: Money Market	4%
Bonds Fixed Income	17%
Inflation Adjusted bonds (TIP)	6%
Equities Domestic (SPY, DIA)	33%
REITS (IYR,RWX)	3%
Mid-cap (MDY)	5%
Small cap (IWM)	4%
Equities Global (EEM, EFA)	24%
Precious Metals, Commod. (GDX, DBA)	4%

As an aggressive investor your time horizon is longer. The assumption is that you can tolerate short-term market volatility. The allocation should also be adjusted to market conditions (bull, neutral or bear markets) and changes in Asset Allocation based on the outlook for domestic *and global equity, fixed income and currency markets*

In addition to adjustments in asset allocation based on investor's risk tolerance (conservative, moderate and aggressive), changes in asset allocation should be influenced by changes in the outlook for domestic and global equity, fixed income and currency markets. Are you more bullish on stocks and bearish on bonds or are you more bullish on bonds and bearish on stocks? Do you expect large-cap stocks to outperform small-cap stocks? Do you expect growth stocks to outperform value stocks? Do you expect developed markets to outperform emerging markets? Which International countries aremore attractive? Do you expect high yield bonds to outperform investment grade bonds? Should you allocate a larger percentage of assets to international (non-U.S.) bonds or to domestic bonds? Is cash more attractive? Asset allocation is a dynamic process and should change as your outlook changes.

Changes in Annual Performance of Indexes.

The need to adjust your asset allocation as market conditions changes is illustrated in the following example. It is not unusual for the best performing fund in one year to become the worst performing fund in another year. Emerging Market MSCI was the best performer in 2003 after being the worst performer in 1998. The RUSSELL 1000 Growth was the best performer in 1998 but was the second worst performer in 2002.

RUSSELL 1000 GROWTH		EMERGING MAKETS MSCI
1998	+38.7 %**	-25.3%***
1999	+33.1%	+66.4%
2000	-22.4%	-30.6%***
2001	-20.4%	- 2.47%

2002	-27.9%	- 6.0%
2003	+29.8%	+56.3%****
2004	+ 6.3%	+26.0%****
2005	+ 5.3%	+34.5% ****
2006	+ 9.1%	+32.6%****

** Best performer Index in 1998

*** Emerging Markets MSCI was worst performer Index in 1998, 2000

**** Emerging Markets MSCI was best performer Index in 2003, 2004, 2005, 2006

For the years 1998 to 2006 the worst performing Indexes kept changing

1998	MSCI Eemerging Markets	-25.3%
1999	LB Govt./Cred	- 2.2%
2000	MSCI Emerging Markets	-30.6%
2001	MSCI EAFE	-21.5%
2002	Russell 2000 Growth	-30.3%
2003	LB Intermed Gov/Cred	+ 4.3%
2004	LB Intermed Gov/Cred	+ 3.0%
2005	LB Intermed Gov/Cred	+ 1.6%
2006	LB Govt./Cred	+ 3.8%

LB Intermed. Gov. bonds were the worst performing index in 2003, 2004 and 2005 Source MSCI, S & P,

Small-cap ETFs are an important tool in asset allocation. Over the years, several times the Dow Jones Industrials – which represents the big stocks — performed better than the small-cap sector, (IJR) which represents the small stocks. During other periods, the small-cap sector outperformed the (DIA) by about 10%. From January 1, 2001, to December 31, 2002, the DIA underperformed iShares S&P Small-Cap 600 index fund (IJR). For the two-year period (January 1, 2001 to December 31, 2002), the small-cap growth sector (DSG) underperformed the small-cap value (DSV). During those two years, the best index to own was the small-cap value. DSG dropped by about 40%, while DSV was unchanged.

Rebalancing of asset allocation

Rebalancing is an ongoing process. Rebalancing is bringing your portfolio back to its original asset allocation mix. Different sectors of the market will fluctuate at different times at different rates within different trends. This will impact your intended asset allocation. In order to maintain your desired asset allocation you may sell some appreciated assets to bring the portfolio back to your normalized allocation which has been customized to your needs. Your allocation may be subject to legal constraints, tax considerations, your age, income needs, estate planning and your target rate of return. The percentage of asset allocation may have to be rebalanced when one asset class rises in value and accounts for a higher percentage value than its desired target allocation.

For example: Take a portfolio valued at $100,000 with moderate investment objective and a target percentage allocation of: bonds 20%, SPY 20%, DIA 20%, MDY 10%, QQQ 10%, IJR 10% and EFA 10%. The ETF (QQQ) rises in value from $10,000 to $12,000. The total portfolio value is now equal to $102,000. You wish to maintain the original target allocation of QQQ at 10% of the portfolio's value. The new allocation to QQQ is now 10% of $102,000 or $10,200. Then all the other allocations have to be rebalanced. From the increased value of $2,000, you have to sell $1,800 worth of QQQ and buy $400 of bonds, $400 worth of SPY, $400 worth of DIA, $200 worth of MDY, $200 worth of IJR and $200 worth of EFA. The new values of the allocations will be:

Bonds	SPY	DIA	MDY	QQQ	IJR	EFA	TOTAL
20%	20%	20%	10%	10%	10%	10%	100%
$20,400	$20,400	$20,400	$10,200	$10,200	$10,200	$10,200	$102,000

You should be aware of the extent of correlation between the sectors in your portfolio.

Two sectors which are highly correlated do not give you the desired diversification since they fluctuate in the same direction. For example you should not have two sectors which drop in value when interest rates go up. The rebalancing process provides you with a strategy of selling on strength and buying in weakness. Small-cap ETFs are an important part in asset allocation. Over the years, sometimes the Dow Jones Industrials – which represents the big stocks — performs better than the small-cap sector, (IJR) which represents the small stocks. During other periods, the small-cap sector outperformed the (DIA) by about 10%. From January 1, 2001, to December 31, 2002, the DIA underperformed iShares S&P Small-Cap 600 index fund (IJR). For the two-year period (January 1, 2001 to December 31, 2002), the small-cap growth sector (DSG) underperformed the small-cap value (DSV). During those two years, the best index to own was the small-cap value. (DSG) dropped by about 40%, while (DSV) was unchanged.

CHAPTER 5

OPTIONS STRATEGIES

The volume of trading in options is enormous. In the U.S. options now trade on six different exchanges with about 75,000 different quotes per second. There are many options strategies that can help you to take advantage when different markets are moving in different directions. This chapter describes different option strategies several of which are speculative and involve high levels of risk and other that are conservative and involve relatively low levels of risk. Options are also used as a tool to shift risk. It is taking risk on one hand and offsetting risk with the other hand.

Standardized Options

An option is an agreement between a buyer and a seller to buy or sell an underlying asset at a fixed price . That agreement expires on a specific date. Standardized equity options, which are very popular today, started trading on the CBOE in 1973. Today standardized option contracts on individual stocks, equity indexes, government bonds, precious metals and futures contracts trade world-wide on at some 57 exchanges in 27 countries.

When using options strategies as a tool to achieve your investment objectives, both as a seller/writer or as a buyer/holder of options, you must understand both your rights and obligations regarding the potential risks and rewards associated with each specific option strategy. When you invest in options, you can determine the risks you want to take or the risk you want to avoid. You can measure the maximum potential loss or profit of any options strategy you employ. There are three basic reasons to use options as a tool in your investment strategy:

1. Earn additional income (option premium)
2. Portfolio protection
3. Leverage (speculative investments)

Descriptive terms for Options

There are six terms that describe an option.

1. *Option type* (call options and put options). The buyer (owner) of an option has certain rights and obligations. The seller (writer) of an option has certain rights and obligations. The owner of an option has the right but not the obligation to exercise. The seller (writer) of an option has the obligation to accept an exercise if the owner of the option wishes to exercise.

2. *The type of underlying asset.* Options are bought and sold on individual stocks such as IBM, stock indexes and ETFs such as DIA or QQQ, currencies, precious metals, government bonds and future contracts.

3. *Strike price or exercise price* (the price at which the owner of the contract can exercise the option.

4. *Expiration date* (The date on which the right to exercise expires).

5. Exercise style (American or European). American style options can be exercised at any time up to expiration date. European style options can be exercised only on expiration date.

6. *Contract unit* (The contract unit for individual stocks is 100 shares). An owner of one call option with a strike price of $20 has the right to buy 100 shares at $20 per share ($2000.00).

Options Symbols and codes.

Option quotes follow a pattern that enables you to construct and interpret symbols. The basic parts of an option symbol areroot symbol + month code + strike price code The root symbol describing the option is not always the same as the ticker symbol.

Figure 5.1 Options Symbols
Expiration Month Codes

	Jan	Feb	Mar	Apr	May	Jun	Jul	Aug	Sep	Oct	Nov	Dec
Calls	A	B	C	D	E	F	G	H	I	J	K	L
Puts	M	N	O	P	Q	R	S	T	U	V	W	X

Code	Strike Prices					
A	5	105	205	305	405	505
B	10	110	210	310	410	510
C	15	115	215	315	415	515
D	20	120	220	320	420	520
E	25	125	225	325	425	525
F	30	130	230	330	430	530
G	35	135	235	335	435	535
H	40	140	240	340	440	540
I	45	145	245	345	445	545
J	50	150	250	350	450	550
K	55	155	255	355	455	555
L	60	160	260	360	460	560
M	65	165	265	365	465	565
N	70	170	270	370	470	570
O	75	175	275	375	475	575
P	80	180	280	380	480	580
Q	85	185	285	385	485	585
R	90	190	290	390	490	590

S	95	195	295	395	495	595
T	100	200	300	400	500	600
U	7.5	37.5	67.5	97.5	127.5	157.5
V	12.5	42.5	72.5	102.5	132.5	162.5
W	17.5	47.5	77.5	107.5	137.5	167.5
X	22.5	52.5	82.5	112.5	142.5	172.5
Y	27.5	57.5	87.5	117.5	147.5	177.5
Z	32.5	62.5	92.5	122.5	152.5	182.5

Option Expirations cycles

The options cycles are sequence of expiration dates.

January cycle: Jan., April, July, October

February cycle: Feb., May, August, November

March Cycle: March, June, September, December

At present all options have current month and the following month expiration available.

How calls and puts options work.

There are two types of options: call options and put options. A call option is an option contract (between the buyer and the seller) that gives the owner the right (but not the obligation) to buy the underlying security at a specified price (strike price). This right expires on expiration date. The seller of a call option has an obligation to sell the underlying stock if the option is assigned. The seller's obligation also expires on expiration date.

A put option is an option contract gives the owner (buyer) the right to sell the underlying stock at a specified price (strike price) for a fixed period of time until expiration date. The seller (writer) of a put option has the right to collect premium but has the obligation to buy the underlying stock from the option owner if the option is assigned.

Covered and uncovered options

As a covered call option seller, you own the underlying shares as long as you remainobligated to deliver the stock upon assignment. You are subject to all the risks of an owner of the stock (such as declining market prices). You can deliver the stock. You don't have to buy the stock as is the case when you are not covered. Selling covered calls is basically a conservative strategy, while selling uncovered calls is highly speculative. When you are not covered you can either buy back the call (potentially at a substantial loss) to close the open short call position or buy the stock in the open market (at potentially much higher prices), which may result in substantial losses. When you sell uncovered calls, there is no limit to your potential losses. When you sell covered puts you have the cash or buying power to pay for the securities assigned to you under your obligations as a put seller. When you sell uncovered puts, you risk facing margin requirements and substantial risks during periods of declining prices. Selling uncoveredputs is highly speculative and risky.

Value of Options and Levels of Premiums.
(Intrinsic value, time value and volatility)

An option value is made up of "intrinsic value" and "time value". The intrinsic value is the option worth if it is exercised now, or in other words, how much it is "in-the-money". The time value is a function of the time left to expiration. The amount of option premium paid by the buyer and received by the seller is determined by the exchange auctions of supply and demand forces. There are several important factors that determine options prices and values.

A. volatility of the underlying stock

Volatility increases option prices. The higher the volatility, the higher the value (price) that the buyer is willing to pay for options.

B. The time left to expiration (time value)

The more time is left to expiration, the higher the premium level for the option.

C. The difference between the current price of the underlying security and the strike price or exercise price. The more the option price is "out-of the-money", the less valuable is the option. The more the option is "in the money" the more valuable is the options.

D. Market condition and the leverage investors are willing to engage in.
In a speculative market investors are willing to pay relatively higher premiums for options

E. Event driven.
A special event such as merger and acquisition expectations will affect the level of premiums.

Remember, for every buyer of an option there is a seller on the other side. For a transaction to take place, both the buyer and the seller must be satisfied. The buyers have their own reasons why they are buying at a specific moment and a specific price, and the sellers have their own reasons why they wish to sell at the same specific moment and at the same specific price.

Opening and Closing Transactions (Get in and get out of your contract)

You can buy an option to open, or you can buy an option to close. When you buy a call to open, you buy a new option or you add to an existing call position. When you buy a call to close, you buy to cover a short call position. You get out of your contract when you sell an option. If it is an existing option that you sold, you sell to close your position. You sell to open if it is a new option You can always get out of short call position. Assuming that you own a stock and you sold a covered call to open. If you do not wish to get assigned for example and you do not want to be called and sell the stock, you can buy back the call to close.

Dividends and Options

You are entitled to receive dividends when you are the owner of the underlying securities. As a covered writer of call options, you continue to receive dividends as long as you own the underlying securities (when you are covered). You should watch for ex-dividend dates because the owner of the call may exercise the option just prior to ex-dividend date, for the purpose of collecting the dividend. When you own a call option (long) you are not entitled to the dividend. After the ex-dividend date, the price of the underlying security will decline and so will the price of the call option. The price of the put option will rise after the ex-dividend date.

Options as a Tool for Hedging and the transfer of risk

A hedge is the purchase and sale of securities likely to rise and fall in opposite direction under the same condition. For example: The purchase of a stock or an ETF (a long equity position) and the sale of a call option (a short call option position) together with a buy of a put option (a long put option position) is a hedged position. In a hedge, potential profits are sacrificed in order to reduce the level of risk. Customized option strategies are often limited by market liquidity, size of the transaction and regulatory considerations such as post-merger shorting, margin requirements and assignments of call or put options.

OPTIONS STRATEGIES CALLS

Selling (Writing) Covered Call Options
(Short Covered Call Positions)

Writing covered calls is considered one of the most conservative equity investment strategies. It is allowed by the U.S. government as an investment strategy in IRA and 401K accounts. You can write covered calls against your existing stock portfolio or write calls together with a new stock purchase.

The main objectives of selling call options are:

1. To receive additional income on the securities in your portfolio. The additional income equals the amount of call premium received.

2. To partially protect your portfolio against capital losses. You reduce the downside risk inherent in owning a security. Your downside protection is equal to the amount of premium received.

3. To achieve a more stable and consistent investment performance over a long period of time. This is achieved through the reduction in performance volatility.

4. To increase the total return on investment (dividend income plus option income plus potential capital gains income), while reducing the level of risk. When you sell a covered call option, you continue to own the underlying stock. You fully participate in any further gains in the value of the stock up to the strike price. As long as you own the underlying stocks, you are entitled to receive dividends paid to shareholders of the underlying stock. The disadvantage of selling a covered call is that you remain exposed to the downside price risk of the underlying stock, and you do not participate in any gains beyond the call strike price.

5. It is a way to enter a GTC (good till canceled) sell order for the underlying securities, assuming that the option will be exercised at the "out of the money" strike price. If the call option expires without being exercised, you can sell a new call option with a new strike price and a new expiration date. The timing of the sale of call options depends on the expected future behavior of the underlying stock. You are more inclined to sell a call option when you expect the underlying stock to show little price changes over the life of the call option. Tax consideration—short-term and

long-term — may also affect the timing of the sale of the call.

Many ETFs do not have listed options. Several have only highly correlated available options. When you invest in an ETF with the intention of selling a covered call, make sure that listed options are available for that specific ETF. For example: For the Consumer Staple Sector there are several funds. Consumer Dow Jones iShares (IYK) has listed options, Vanguard Consumer Staples VIPERS (VDC) has listed options, but Consumer Staples(KXI) the S&P Global Consumer Staples does not have listed options. The choice would be to buy those ETFs that do have listed options (IYK) or (VDC).

Buy Write CBOE S&P 500 indexes (Covered Calls)

The CBOE publishes two BuyWrite indexes; the (BXM) and the (BXY). The (BXM) uses a strategy of buying the S&P 500 and selling at-the-money calls with one month to expiration. The (BXY) uses the same methodology as the (BXM), but is calculated using a 2% out-of-the-money S&P 500 call options, rather than at-the-money (SPX) call options. The objective of both indexes is to enhance returns and reduce risks. A twenty year performance test indicates that the (BXM) produced annualized returns of 11.8% and a standard deviation of 9.2% and the (BXY) produced an annual return of 12.8% and an 11.0% standard deviation.

Selling (Writing) Naked Calls (Short Uncovered Call Positions)

As a seller of options your aim is to sell time value. The potential maximum gain for the writer of uncovered calls is the premium received. The potential maximum loss is unlimited. Substantial risk exists due to the seller's obligation, should the underlying security rise sharply, and the call is subject to assignment. There is no limit to how high the security's price could rise. An investor who sells naked calls hopes that price behavior of the underlying security is either neutral or slightly bearish.

When you sell a call option you sell the rights to the appreciation in the underlying   Securities above the option exercise price in exchange for the premium received. When you sell uncovered calls you usually sell "out-of the-money" calls.

Buying Call Options (Long Calls)

Buying call options is one of the most popular (but speculative) option strategy. The main attractiveness of a long call strategy is that the percentage gain relative to the premium investment can be significant. The maximum loss is defined and is equal to the premium paid, while the maximum gain is unlimited. The call buyer usually plans to sell the call option at a profit and not necessarily wait until expiration. However the owner of the call contract has fewer and fewer days left to be right as time gets closer to expiration.

The buyer of a call has a "need for speed" to achieve a profitable trade. The "time decay" works against the option buyer. The owner of a "long" option requires that the underlying stock move more than the cost of the option.

Establishing a Bear Call Spread (Buy a Call option and Sell a Call with a lower price)

A bear call spread is a vertical spread. You buy a call (long) and you sell a call (short) with the same expiration date but with different strike prices. The long call strike price is above the short call strike price. For example: Long 75 call, short 70 call. The maximum gain is equal to the net premium received. The maximum loss is equal to The high strike price minus the low strike price minus the net premium received.

Establishing a Bull Call Spread (Buy a Call option and Sell a Call with a higher price)

A bull call spread is a vertical spread. You buy a call (long) and you sell a call (short) against it with the same expiration date but with different strike prices. The long call strike is below the short call strike. It is a "cash debit" transaction since the long call costs more than the short call. Maximum gain is equal to (high strike price - Low strike – net premium paid). Maximum loss is equal to net premium paid.

The call you sell to open helps to reduce the cost of the more valuable option you are buying as the money you collect on the short calls will be money that you collect as soon as the trade is executed. Bull calls spreads are excellent for making a bullish play on the underlying stock. You define the profit and loss potential when the trade is initiated.

You also reduce the cost of the long call. A sudden increase in call buying volume may indicate activity by knowledgeable investors who expect the underlying stock to rise. For this activity to be statistically significant the daily volume should exceed the option open interest.

Buy a call option and sell two calls with a higher strike price

Another bull spread strategy to consider is to buy one call option and selling two calls with a higher strike price. The "cash credit" from the two calls will pay for the "cash debit" of the call purchased.

Establishing a calendar spread

When you expect the market to move gradually up or down you establish a calendar spread by buying the longer-term option and selling the shorter-term option with the same strike price.

You take advantage of the non-linear nature of the time decay. As you get closer to expiration the time decay is faster.

PUTS

Selling (Writing) Covered Put Options (Short Covered Put Positions) (Willing to own the underlying securities)

The selling (not buying) of put options strategy has been a favorite strategy of professional traders for many years. Selling options instead of buying options is moving the odds in your favor. It is well established that about 80% of all options sold and held to expiration expire worthless (out of the money).

The objectives of selling covered put options are:

1. Your rights as a seller of puts is to earn income which is equal to the amount of premium received. (Your obligation is to buy the underlying stock at exercise price upon assignment.)

2. When you sell a put you are taking on the obligation to buy a stock often as part of a plan to buy the underlying stock below current market prices. You often select an exercise price at or below levels at which you believe the stock is attractive for purchase. In a way, it is a "good till expiration" order to buy the stock as a price limit below the current market price. (One put option is a contract for 100 shares of the underlying stock. Ten put options are a contract for 1000 shares.)

As a put writer, you enter into an obligation to buy the underlying stock at the stock price and by expiration date. Your net buying cost is reduced by the amount of put premium received. When you sell a covered put, you should have the amount of cash you need to pay for the underlying stock in case of assignment. You can invest this cash reserve in Treasury bills or other short-term fixed-income securities. To terminate your short put obligation, you can buy back the put "to close".

You can also roll over the put obligation to the future by buying back to close the outstanding short put and selling a new short put to open with a new expiration date. The rollover will generate additional credit income (time value). The credit income is equal to the net difference between the cost of buying the outstanding put "to close" and the proceeds from selling the new put "to open." One of the advantages of selling puts as a way to buy the stock below the market is that you do not have to lay out the money to buy the stock when you enter into the short put obligation. Selling covered puts is considered a conservative investment strategy. There are situations, when the investor is bullish on the underlying stock, that selling a put option will be a profitable transaction, but buying a call option will result in a loss.

For example: A stock is trading at 40 and you bought a call for $1.50 with a strike price of 40. Should the stock rise to $41, you would still lose money. The stock has to rise to 41.5 for you to break even. However, the seller of a put will make money under the same conditions. As a buyer of options you need "perfect timing" to make a profit. As a seller of options you have an advantage since you don't have to be absolutely correct in predicting short-term market moves.

Selling Uncovered Puts (Short Uncovered Puts)

An uncovered put writer enters into a bullish bet that the stock will rise. You have no desire to own the underlying stock. You expect the put to expire worthless. The maximum loss could be substantial. It is equal to the strike price minus premium received. The maximum gain for the writer of uncovered puts is the premium received.

Selling cash secured Puts

Selling cash secured puts is a way to ultimately buying the underlying securities at a desired target price. This target price is below current price. It can also be used just as a way to collect premiums. Writing options as a strategy is not a day trading strategy. Assuming days left to expiration of about 30-60 days most of the activity will take place near expiration dates. Open options positions can be closed at any time

Stock price near strike price just prior to expiration date

When the stock price is near the strike price just prior to expiration date, you have several alternative actions. You can do nothing and hope that the put option will expire.

You can close your open position and buy the put. You can roll over to next month – buying the current month to close and selling the next month to open

Establishing credit put spreads

When you sell the higher strike price put and buy the lower strike price put you receive a net premium credit.

Buying Put Options (Long Puts) / Buy Insurance

When you buy insurance you give away cash and give away risk. When an insurance company sells insurance they accept cash and they accept risk. As an owner of a put option, you hope for a significant downturn in the price of the underlying stock. Your maximum loss is the premium paid. Your maximum gain is the strike price minus the premium paid. Many investors plan to sell the put at a profit before expirations, while other investors exercise the put and sell the underlying stock.

You may buy a put to protect an existing stock position. This is similar to buying an insurance policy. Buying a put is an expense and so is buying an insurance policy. It is an expense well spent if the underlying stock drops sharply or if you collect on an insurance policy. Buying protective puts on an ETF is an efficient tool in managing portfolio risks. When you own a put option, you benefit from a decline in securities prices. Prices of put options will rise when prices of the underlying securities fall. You can buy put options to protect unrealized gains in your current stock position. This will guarantee a selling price as long as the put option is outstanding. Your investment will also participate in additional capital gains if the underlying securities continue to rise. Yet, you will maintain full price protection below the strike price of the put.

One of the disadvantages of buying put options is that you must pay a premium (cost of the option) as well as the fact that the option loses all its value on expiration date. You also have a downside exposure up to the out-of-the-money strike price. After the expiration date you may buy new put options, but that will require a new cost to pay the premium. Buying puts has an advantage over selling short since the potential loss is limited to the cost of the put. Selling short has no expiration date but it involves a very high level of risk since the potential loss on a short position is unlimited and you may be forced to cover your short at a substantial loss. The cost of puts tend to decline after an extended rise in the market and tend to rise after an extended decline in the market as interest in buying puts by speculators is going up and put premiums will go up as well. The choice of expiration dates and strike prices is a function of costs of premiums and your outlook for the market behavior.

Combination Strategies

The following combination strategy has a favorable risk/reward profile relative to an equity index (such as the S&P 500) and bonds. Its performance falls between intermediate bonds and equities. The strategy known as "COLLAR Strategy" involves:

Buy a stock, sell a call option and buy a put option.

A. Buy a stock.

B. Sell out-of-the-money call option to generate current additional income from premiums and establish a potential capital gain.

C. Buy out-of-the-money put option to protect the portfolio from a significant market decline over a short period of time..

(Part of the money received from selling the call is used to buy puts).

The above combination strategy is a tool to achieve a substantial reduction in portfolio volatility and a steady above-average return from dividend income plus the net credit from the selling the calls minus the cost of buying the puts and the potential for realized capital gains (the out-of-the-money portion of the calls). The objective is to receive income from three sources: dividend income, capital gains income, and options income. This strategy has a favorable risk/reward ratio. It captures part of the return associated with the equity index while exposing investors to only part of the risk associated with the index volatility. The maximum gain is equal to the (call strike price plus premium received for the call) minus (stock purchase price minus premium paid for the put). The maximum loss is equal to the (stock purchase price plus premium paid for the put) minus (put strike plus premium received for the call).

One simple way to explain this combination strategy is to compare it to thepurchase of income-producing real estate properties.

Combination Option Strategy	Real Estate Investment	
INVESTMENT	Buy a stock or an	Buy real estate properties
ETF Index		
INCOME	Sell call options	Rent the properties
	Receive call premium	Collect rental income

EXPENSES	Buy put options	Buy insurance
	Cost of put premium	Cost of insurance premium

The above option strategy will perform better than the market in a down market and will perform worse than the market in an up market. This will result in a less volatile portfolio. The above option strategy can also be used when a portfolio is concentrated in one equity position. For example, company executives may have a large portion of their portfolio invested in the company's stock. The objectives involved in using the above combination option strategy in a highly concentrated equity position are:

To defer recognition of capital gains taxes.

To comply with existing regulatory restriction on selling concentrated positions.

The need for cash by the owner of the stock.

The need for income beyond the cash dividends

To lower a concentrated position of market risk, change of management risk and overall industry risk.

To protect the portfolio from a potential big decline.

To diversify a personal portfolio

The above option strategy could be executed in such a way that there will be no need to invest additional money. This means that selling the calls will produce enough income to buy the puts. This is also called zero premium protective collars.

Establishing a short Straddle Selling put (short put) plus Selling calls (short calls) combination strategy

The objective of a short straddle — selling puts and selling calls simultaneously is to collect two premiums. The investor collect the premium from the calls as well as from the puts. On the other hand, the investor enters into two obligations. As the writer of an uncovered put, one is obligated to buy, at strike price, the underlying security if assigned to you by the put owner. As the writer of an uncovered call, one is obligated to deliver the underlying security if called by the owner of the call. In a short, uncovered call position, one's maximum loss is unlimited. In a short, uncovered put position, the maximum loss is substantial and is equal to the strike price minus premium received. It is a profitable strategy when the stock moves sideways.

Establishing a short Option Strangle

A strangle is selling both a call and a put at the same time. The put is sold out-of-the money below current price of the underlying stock and the call is sold out-of-the-money above the current stock price. If the price of the underlying stock is between the two strike prices by expiration date, both options will expire worthless. The total profits are equal to both premiums collected. It is more conservative than only sell a call strategy because part or all the loss on one side will be offset with gains on the other side of the strangle. The time decay works in your favor on both side of the strangle.

Index Options

All index options are cash-settled. This means that index options are settled through the payment of cash, rather than securities. You should be aware that the exercise settlement value of an index option that is derived from the opening prices of the constituent securities may not be reported for several hours following the opening of trading in those securities. Trading in index options involve special risks. Writers of cash-settled index call options cannot provide in advance for their potential settlement obligations by acquiring and holding the underlying interest. Timing risks makes spread positions and multiple option strategies involving cash-settled American style index options substantially riskier than similar strategies involving physical delivery options. (For other risks, see "Characteristics and Risks of Standardized Options" publication, published by CBOE.) Some index options are European- style options.

OEX S&P 100 Index Options

OEX options represent one of the largest index option products in the world in terms of volume. OEX options are American-style, meaning that an option holder may exercise options at any time prior to expiration date.

Order Execution Risk – don't chase an option price

An important part of buying and selling options is the execution of orders. When you try to execute a sell put transaction should you hit the bid price?, should you place your order between the bid and the asked? or should you just place a limit order?. Generally speaking you should not chase an option price. You should select the option price that will achieve your minimum expected rate of return. It is very important to evaluate the trading volume activity of an option and the spread between the bid and asked prices.

When the spread is large between the bid and asked it is difficult to execute " rolling over" from one month to another orders. Execution problems will also reduce the expected rate of return. This additional execution risk should be evaluated when you select alternative underlying securities and ETFs as potential investments.

Market Volatility and collecting options premiums

Investors can use market volatility to their advantage. The higher the volatility, the more you collect from premiums. As of 2006, the market in general can be described as schizophrenic and a roller-coaster ride, But this higher volatility with higher premiums can be used to one's advantage. You should distinguish between prolonged down trends in prices and frequent up-and-down price changes, The objective is not necessarily to own the underlying securities. The investment objective is to collect the premiums.

However, since you are exposed to buy the securities upon assignment, be sure that you are willing to own and buy the underlying securities at the strike price minus the premium collected. Those decisions are often based on a combination of technical and fundamental analysis. Volatility can change and often does change. In the long run, prices of the underlying securities reflect fundamental factors. Therefore you should be familiar with the fundamentals of the securities you trade.

Cash Secured Put Return Calculations Worksheet

Security name: Symbol: Current price:

Strike Price: Option Premium:

Expiration Month: Days to Expiration:

Initial Cash-Secured Required

1. Sell................Puts @............. ._____

(# of puts x Premium x 100)

2. Less option commission

_____

3. Net Proceeds from Put Sale

_____

4. Deposit cash for Stock (ETF) Potential Purchase

_____

(# of puts x 100 x Strike Price)

5. Total cash required (Line 4 less Line 3)

_____

If Option Expires (Not Assigned)

(Stock above strike Price)

6. Retain Net Premium. (Line 3) = Net Profit

_____

7. Percentage Return for period

_____

(Line 6 divided by Line 5)

8. Annualized Return

_____

(%) Return x 365 divided by # of Days to Expiration)

If Options Assigned (Buy Stock)

(Stock Price Below Strike Price)

9. Buy..........Shares @ Strike........

_____

10. Plus stock Commission

_____

11. Less Net Option Premium (Line 3)

_____

12. Net cost of stock Position

_____

(Line 9 + Line 10 – Line 11)

13. Breakeven   (Line 12 divided by # of Shares)

_____

Covered Writes Options Calculation Worksheet

Security Name and Symbol:_____

Option:_Call   __Month:_____Strike price:_____

Annual Dividend:_____Ex-dividend dates_____

Expiration Date:_____Days to Expiration:_____

Initial Investment Required:

A. Purchase # Shares:_____@Price:_____Total_____

B. Plus Stock Commission_____

C. Total Stock Purchase cost (A+B)_____

D. Option Premium (# Contracts_____@_Price_____) Total___

E. Less Option Commissions_____

F. Net proceeds from sale of option (D – E)_____

G. Net Investment:_(C – F)_____

H. Breakeven Point:(G – dividends) divided by # of Shares _____

Profit Potential if Stock is called on Expiration Date:

I. Sell _____ Shares @ Strike Price:_____ Total :   _____

J. Less Stock commission: _____ _____

K. Plus #____ Dividends on #_____Shares   _____

L. Total Proceeds (I – J + K)_____

M. Less net Investment (G)   _____

N. Net Profits for period: (L – M)_____

O. Percentage Return for period (Line N divided by Line M)

_____

P. Annualized (%) Return: (% Return for the period (O) x 365
Divided by Days to
Expiration_____

Profit Potential – Assume Stock Price is Unchanged

A. Option premium _____

B. Less Option Commissions _____

C. Less buy stock commission _____

D. Plus Dividends _____

E. Net profits (A – B – C + D) _____

F. Net Investment (M) _____

G. Percentage Returned for the period _____

H. Annualized percentage return (G) x 365 divided by Days to Exp.____

CHAPTER 6

A DYNAMIC ETFs EQUITY INCOME STRATEGY (COLLECTING PUTS AND CALLS PREMIUMS) A CORE / SATELLITE INVESTMENT STRATEGY

Objective of the Core / Satellite strategy

To achieve absolute double digits returns in various market conditions with low levels of volatility and without excessive risk of capital regardless of the direction of the securities market. Absolute returns are defined as positive total returns, regardless of the direction of securities markets. The aim is to provide added income and lessen portfolio volatility in order to improve returns on investments, and at the same time, reduce the risk of losses during periods of a market decline.

To achieve the stated objectives, a core investment strategy that involves tracking the CBOE put index (PUT) and the BuyWrite index (BUX) is employed. This core strategy involves primarily the selling of put options and covered call options on the S&P 500.In addition, a satellite investment strategy that primarily involves selling put options and covered call options on selected ETFs is also employed.

Several ETFs do not have listed options. In those situation, options can be sold on the top holdings of individual securities within the selected ETFs. Available cash is invested in short-term governments and investment grade corporate fixed income securities. The portfolio's expected total return is based on income generated from five sources:

1. Income from selling put options.
2. Income from selling call options.
3. Income from dividends on equities.
4. Income from interest on fixed income securities.
5. Net capital gains from investments.

The average expected annual return of the core strategy (net after fees and expenses) and without using leverage is expected to be about 12%. Additional income averaging about 4% is expected to be produced by the Satellite ETF equity income strategy. This 16% expected total return is currently more than triple the return on 10 year treasuries. When leverage is used the average annual return could further be increased. The portfolio's expected return is measured against two market benchmarks; the Russell 3000 and the yield on 10 years treasuries.

The Core Investment Strategy

The core investment strategy involves selling one month "at the money" put options tracking the CBOE S&P 500 put index (PUT) and selling one month "at the money" covered call options tracking the CBOE S&P 500 BuyWrite monthly index (BXM).

The Satellite Investment Strategy

The satellite strategy involves primarily the selling of puts and calls on selected ETFs. The objective of that strategy is to increase the rate of return and to reduce portfolio volatility as measured by standard deviation.. Managing and mitigating risks is achieved by diversification of exposures to ETFs with different betas and different correlations. The satellite strategy also involves the tracking of the S&P 500 2% out-of-the-money BuyWrite index (BXY).

Time Decay

We are all familiar with the expression "time is money". Writing options is a good example that time is indeed money. The strategy of selling puts is attractive because "time is on your side". It involves the concept of "TIME DECAY". (It resembles the phenomena of melting ice cubes). The value of the option declines as less time is left to expiration. The useful life of an option decreases as we get closer to expiration. A one week option is worth less than a two weeks option. Furthermore, the speed of the decline in the value of the option accelerates as it gets closer to expiration date. Selling options instead of buying options improve the odds in your favor. It is estimated that about 80% of all options sold expire worthless.

Expiration Dates and Strike Prices

Puts options that expire in one months are sold to take advantage of the acceleration in "time decay". When an option expires in 30 days, you need to forecast the volatility of the underlying securities only for that short-term time period. You don't have to forecast where the underlying stock may trade several years later. On occasion, options with longer expiration dates are sold because of factors such as ex-dividend dates, expected announcements, merger plans or changes in the composition of an index. Usually the strike prices should be close to "at-the-money" price. However, in an up market strike price should be "in–the–money" and in a down market strike prices should be "out-of-the-money". The choice of strike prices may also be near technical support or resistance levels, near the 80 day moving average or at a price where the put open interest is relatively high. When the stock price is near the strike price just prior to expiration date you have several possible alternative actions. Do nothing and hope that the put option will expire. Close your open position by buying the written put. Roll over to next month by buying the current month to close and selling the next month to open.

Options "rolling" to next month

As options expirations date is getting closer, the probability of an assignment has to be evaluated. In a situation when it looks like the put option will be assigned (the option is " in the money") a "rolling over" to the next month expiration should be considered. When you "roll over", you close the current month option and you open the next month option usually with the same strike price. The key consideration is the net credit collected from the additional month time value together with prevention of an assignment.

The advantages of Selling Puts

Selling put options has been a favorite strategy of professional traders for a long time. When you sell a put you have the right to receive a premium, and you have the obligation to buy the underlying securities at a specific price. If the option expires your income is equal to the amount of premium received. If you are assigned, in effect, you buy the underlying securities at a lower price (strike price minus premium received). When you write a put option, you should be familiar with the underlying stock and you should be prepared to buy it upon assignment.

The premium is received immediately when the put is sold and the proceeds from the sale of the put can be invested. This is similar to what is known as a "float" in the insurance business. In implementing the "sell put" core strategy, it is not required that all options outstanding remain open till expiration date. When option price declines (due to increase in the price of the underlying security) it may become profitable to close (buy back) the open position before expiration date.

Volume of listed and OTC Put and call options.

Recently the volume of puts trades has been rising as more portfolio managers are buying puts as an ongoing insurance strategy. Investors, often for tax reasons, may prefer to keep their long positions in the underlying securities and buy puts to protect positions against a market drop. Sellers of puts provide the supply side for a premium received. Inaddition to the daily volume of puts and the open interest volume, you should examine the price spread between the bid and asked prices. When listed options are not available or when the volume of listed option is low, OTC options may be used. To implement an ongoing put option program, a portion of put activity on individual ETFs may be conducted in OTC markets.

Selling Puts and "Buying Securities + Selling calls" (Covered Writing)

When you buy the underlying securities and sell covered calls (a similar strategy to a "sell put" strategy), you enter into two transactions. First, you buy the securities (often at the asked price) and secondly you sell the call option (often at the bid price). Thus, selling puts reduces transaction costs and is a more efficient transaction. Both strategies generate income, raise your portfolio yield and add downside protection.

When the price of the underlying stock drops and the put is "in the money" you may be assigned. Upon assignments you have several alternative actions. You can sell the assigned stock and sell a new put or you can sell a covered call. If and when the probability of assignment is high (an "in the money" condition before expiration) you can roll over the option from the present month to the next collecting net credit for the additional time value.

A short "strangle"

A short strangle is an option position of out-of-the-money puts and out-of-the-money calls with different strike prices but with the same expiration date. In a short strangle both options are written (sold short). When the probability is high that the underlying stock will remain within the put and call strike prices boundary by expiration date, both options will expire and you collect two premiums. On occasions, the portfolio may include positions of short puts long underlying securities and short calls.

A "collar" option strategy

You establish a spread strategy which involves buying an "out of the money" protective put option. and selling out of the money call option. When the spread is established, the price of the underlying stock is above the put strike price and below the call strike price. It is used to protect the underlying stocks in the portfolio during periods of market decline. When and if the call option expires, you can sell a new call option at a new strike price. If the stock price moves up, the call strike price can be established at a higher strike price. The money that was collected from selling the calls is used to pay the premium for the puts.

The use of Leverage

The strategy of selling options may or may not involve the use of leverage even when the trades are booked in a margin account. Cash reserves (against which the options are written) including investments in short-term fixed income securities is used as a source of funds to meet potential assignment obligations. However, the use of leverage when taking advantage of lower securities prices and higher put premiums during a market decline will increase the expected rate of return.

Collecting "Insurance" Premiums

When an insurance company sells insurance it accepts cash and also accepts risk. When you buy insurance you give away cash and you give away risk. The buyer of a put option often takes this step as an insurance to protect the portfolio against a potential market drop. In effect the buyer "buys" an insurance policy for which he is willing to pay an insurance premium. The seller of a put option is in effect selling an insurance policy for which insurance premium is collected. In the insurance business, you have to sell a large number of insurance policies (based on actuarial calculations) to reduce your risk exposure to insurance obligations. Similarly, diversification of underlying securities exposure with positions for the seller of puts is therefore of great importance to reduce the downside risk in a period of market decline.

The investment strategy used for ETFs that do not have "listed" options.

The S&P 500 has very active listed options and many other ETFs have listed options. However, several ETFs have inactive listed options with large spreads between bid and asked prices or do not have listed options at all. To implement the put writing strategy, ETF call and put options activity mat be conducted in OTC markets.

Options can also be sold on the top holdings of individual securities within an ETF. Although specific individual stocks are subject to higher volatility than the underlying ETF, the volatility of a basket of the top ten securities holdings should approximate the volatility of the underlying ETF.

Selling options on individual securities.

Options can be sold on individual securities when an ETF does not have listed options.Options on individual securities in may be sold in "event-driven" special situations, when these securities are found to be undervalued and when their market value is below their intrinsic value. A diversified investment portfolio of 25-30 ETFs can be replaced by 250-300 individual securities for which options can be sold. As part of an ongoing strategy, options writing may be conducted in the OTC market.

Strategies for a prolonged bear market

During a prolonged bear market, the portfolio should be exposed to low beta ETFs. Selling puts should be overweight in "out of the money" puts. In addition larger than usual cash position should be kept. Upon assignment of the underlying securities "in the money" calls should be sold. During a rapid decline in securities prices, credit put spreadscan be sold. The gains on the "long" puts will offset some of the losses on the "short" puts. Bearish call spreads can be established. In a bearish call spread you sell simultaneously a call option with a lower strike price and buy another call options with a higher strike price. This will result in a net premium credit. A defensive investment strategy may include Low P/E sectors, High dividend paying sectors, writing puts with strike prices 3-4% out-of the-money and no or little exposure to cyclical sectors.During a prolonged bear market an investment can be made in one or more of Bear Market ETFs. One of the most popular Bear Market ETFs is the (SDS).

(SDS) UltraShort S&P 500 ProShares (AMEX)

Category: Bear Market

(SDS) operates as an ETF. It seeks daily investment results that correspond to twice

(200%) the inverse (opposite) of the daily performance of the S&P 500 Index. (SDS) has

a (-0.99) (minus 0.99) correlation to the S&P 500.

The performance during an unusual "event driven" market drop

In extreme markets, the question is how correlated are the portfolio's ETF holdings and or the put assignment exposures to various sectors. Historically an "event-driven" decline of over 10% is expected to take place in about one out of every 16 months. Since we invest primarily in low beta ETFs together with low correlation ETFs which results in a low level of concentration to risk exposures, the portfolio's decline is expected to be at a much lower percentage than the overall market.

The performance is also a function of the time frame (duration) of the decline and the bounce back reversal that follows. Since performance is usually reported on a monthly basis and since most reversals to the upside take place within a month, the affect on monthly performance is expected to be relatively small.

The performance during a highly improbable Catastrophic Black Swan Event

It is not the intention of the dynamic ETFs option income strategy to completely protect the portfolio during a highly improbable catastrophic event. It is realistic to assume that with some investments in short ETFs, covered calls and long puts, the decline in N.A.V. will be less than the decline in the overall market.

The CBOE S&P 500 BuyWrite Index (BXM) and the CBOE S&P 500 BuyWrite (2%) Out-of–the-Money BuyWrite Index (BXY).

The (BXM) is a 20 years time tested strategy. It has gained acceptance as a conservative strategy. It is a covered call strategy using the S&P 500 and selling at-the-money one month call options. This strategy is used to enhance portfolio returns and reduce volatility. Using a BuyWrite strategy an investor buys a stock or a basket of stocks, and also sells ("writes") call options that correspond to the stock or a basket of stocks.

The (BXY) BuyWrite index is using Out-of-the-Money calls strategy to boost income and Risk-Adjusted Returns. It uses the same methodology as the widely accepted CBOE S&P 500

BUYWrite index (BXM), but is calculated using a 2% Out-of the- Money S&P 500 (SPX) call options. The (BXY) yields lower premiums in return for a greater participation in the upside moves of the S&P 500. The time tested annualized return (before transactions costs, fees and expenses)was 11.9% for the (BXM) and 12.7% for the (BXY). The volatility (standard deviation) for the (BXM) was 9.4% and 11.3% for the (BXY)

A Closed-End fund that employ
options income strategies (ETJ)

Eaton Vance Risk-Managed diversified equity Income fund (ETJ) raised $1.3 billion In an initial public offering. The fund inception date was 07-31-07. For the four months period Aug. 01-07 to Nov. 30-07 the Net Asset Value rose by 5.44% or an average monthly gain of 1.36%.

This closed-end fund primary investment objective is to provide current income with a secondary objective of capital appreciation. The fund seeks to provide less volatile return and reduced exposure to loss of value during a stock market decline. This fund invests in a diversified portfolio of common stocks and employs a variety of puts and calls options strategies. About 50% of the portfolio is invested on the "short" side. The primary objective is to produce capital gains both in up markets and down markets.

A Unique Core / satellite Investment Strategy

The core / satellite strategy employed is unique. It involves both the S&P 500 and many different "Exchange Traded Funds" (ETFs). Most existing funds that use covered calls investment strategies buy "long" equities and selling "short" call options on only one specific index such as the S&P 500. Furthermore, they do not employ risk management strategies to reduce risk of losses during market declines. On the other hand, the dynamic ETF equity income strategy employs a combination of different investment strategies to add income and at the same time reduce volatility and lowering portfolio's beta.

The core / satellite strategy primarily includes:

1. Employ risk management strategies by reducing portfolio's beta and investing in many ETFs with low and or negative correlation..

2. Selling put option to receive premiums and if assigned buy the underlying securities at lower prices. In a steady rising bull market, most of the time the put options will expire.

3. Buy (on assignment) securities that will satisfy risk-averse value investors using sector allocation and diversification models.

4. Selling call options to receive premiums.

The difference between a "market neutral" strategy, Absolute Return strategy and A dynamic ETF equity options income strategy.

In a "market neutral" strategy about 50% of the portfolio is invested on the "long" side and about 50% of the portfolio is invested on the "short" side. The primary objective in a "market neutral" strategy is to produce capital gains whether in up or down markets. This, however, does not guarantee against portfolio losses or that the portfolio will not decline in value either in up or down markets. Although it attempts to produce results that do not depend on the direction of the market, Several of the "long" positions may actually decline and at the same time several of the "short" positions may go up in price. The Lipper index of "market neutral" hedge funds indicates that during the first six months of 2007 the average annual return in "market neutral" funds was only about 5.5% annualized).

In an "absolute return" strategy, a target rate of return is established as a benchmark measurement of performance. The percentage allocation between "long" and "short" positions and the portfolio asset allocation is based on the manager's decision.

The "dynamic ETF equity options income" strategy seeks to produce income both in up and down markets and manage risk by diversification of correlation that results in a low volatility (low beta) portfolio where several holdings go up in value while other holdings in the portfolio decline in value. The emphasis is on income. Capital gain is only a secondary objective. The Dynamic ETF income strategy is not intended to achieve "home runs". It is the monthly incremental income that will produce the overall performance.

The past performance of the S&P 500 "put write index (PUT)

The Chicago board options exchange has back tested data covering the last 20 years showing that the sell put (put write) strategy produced an annual return of 12.6% (before expenses) with lower volatility than a "buy write" strategy and with lower volatility than the underlying index (S&P500). The selling puts strategy involves the selling of one month at the money put options on the S&P500 as a single ETF underlying security.

The past performance of a dynamic ETFs options income strategy- the satellite strategy.

Many ETFs are relatively new and little performance data is available given their "short life" to-date. The historical performance statistics is mostly available on indices such as the S&P 500. Volume of options has risen steadily and the spread between bids and asked has been narrowed.

A CBOE study of past data over a period of 20 years, indicates that a sell "PUT" strategy. selling one month at-the-money puts, resulted in an average annual return of 12.6%.It is reasonable to assume that a strategy that involves a diversified fund with many ETFs with different correlations and different beats should produce a higher absolute average annual rate of return.. It is more than the 12.6% average annual return of the "write put" strategy. A dynamic ETF equity income strategy is expected to have less downside volatility and a lower beta. The portfolio's beta is expected to be equal to about 0.7.

Return and Volatility.

The CBOE 20 year study of the "sell put" strategy indicates that the 12.6 % average return was achieved with an annualized standard deviation of about 8%. This compares to an average return of about 6.5% with an annualized standard deviation of about 5% for the 5-year treasuries and a 12% return for the S&P500 with a 14% standard deviation. In conclusion; the sell "PUT" strategy had a volatility of only slightly above the volatility of 5–year treasuries but the sell put strategy had more than double the return on 5-year treasuries. The sell put strategy had about half of the volatility of the S&P 500.

Annualized Standard Deviation and the Sharpe Ratio

The annualized standard deviation for the 20 year data test was about 8%. This is about 6% lower than the 14% standard deviation for the S&P 500. (lower standard deviation and lower correlation add potential alpha to a core portfolio). The Sharpe ratio which is equal to the "excess return" over the "risk free" return divided by the standard deviation was equal to 1.08. (excess return was equal to 12.6% minus $4.0% or 8.6%) and the annualized standard deviation was equal to 8.0%). The Sharpe ratio is equal to 1.08. (8.6% divided by 8).

Know your Beta

Beta is a measure of a stock volatility relative to the volatility of the market. (market is defined here as the S&P 500) A beta less than 1.0 is less volatile than the market. A diversified portfolio of many ETFs is expected to be less volatile than the overall market. A portfolio of many selected ETFs using a core / satellite strategy is expected to have a beta of about 0.5.to 0.70. Knowing the beta of each holding and the average beta for the whole portfolio is important because it helps you manage and mitigate risk.

Correlation, Asset allocation and Sector Rotation

A portfolio exposed to many ETFs with different correlations will result in several securities going up when other holdings go down in value. Overall portfolio risk is reduced by diversification of asset classes, sectors, indexes and global ETFs. This diversification is a dynamic process that involves asset allocation and sector rotation. The expected overall portfolio correlation to the S&P 500 should be about 0.7.

Downside Volatility and Risk Mitigation

The main element in mitigating risk in both the core S&P 500 strategy and the satellite ETF strategy is the short-term expiration dates for the options sold together with the selection of Exchange Traded Funds. It takes into consideration the "beta" of each ETF and the correlation to the S&P 500. The objective is to construct a portfolio which is "non-directional". Options usually are written "at-the-money". During a bear market "out-of-the-money puts" and "in the money" calls are sold. To protect "long" positions a strategy of stop-loss discipline is also employed.

A twenty year test of "sell put strategy" at the money for one month expiration points to a volatility similar to the volatility of five year treasuries and half of the volatility of the S&P 500. An investment in a diversified portfolio of 20-25 ETFs is expected to further reduce the downside volatility risk. The "selling puts" strategy is not a "day trading" strategy. Although open positions may be closed at any time, most of the sell or buy activity is centered around monthly expiration dates.

A CORE / SATELLITE BLENDED STRATEGY

A "non-managed" Core portion and a Satellite "managed" portion of the total portfolio.

The core "sell put" strategy which tracks the CBOE S&P 500 put index (PUT) and the BuyWrite index (BUX) is the "non-managed" portion of the total portfolio. (The S&P 500 is a "non-managed" Index). Its performance is not dependent on the investment skills of the portfolio manager. The satellite strategy engages in an "ETFs Equity options income" strategy which is used to enhance the rate of return and to reduce the standard deviation (volatility) is the "managed" portion of the portfolio. It attempts to capitalize on market opportunities and does depend to some degree on the manager's investment skills. The core / satellite portfolio is a blended portfolio.

PAST PERFORMANCE IS NO GUARANTEE OF FUTURE RESULTS

CHAPTER 7

INVESTMENT TIMING

The importance of timing decisions

You should distinguish between a fundamental intrinsic value of an operating company, or the relative attractiveness of a sector, or the fundamental appeal of a specific country and the short term price behavior in the open market of a stock or an ETF. The short-term timing decisions for option trading decisions, in, at or out of the money options and strike price decisions, expiration date decisions are short term decisions and investment timing for that time horizon is important.

In life, timing is everything. When investors talk about investment timing and technical indicators, they are really talking about probabilities — The probability of correctly identifying price trends, changes in trends, and market top and bottom. Investment timing is an important key element to successful investing. You may invest in a fundamentally attractive stock or in a promising sector and lose money if you bought it at the "wrong" time. Yet, you may invest in securities with poor fundamentals but still make money if your timing was right. The field of investment timing involves many timing indicators to identify existing trends, changes in trends, and overbought / oversold market conditions. These indicators are used by many investment professionals as an additional tool in making buy, hold and sell decisions. It is very unlikely that at any given point in a market cycle all timing indicators are either bullish or bearish. You will probably find indicators that will give you a bearish signal near a market bottom or a bullish signal near a market top. It is more likely that a majority of timing indicators will indicate a bottom or a top formation and or identify changes in short term, intermediate or long term trends.

From time to time, market indicators have to be recalibrated to account for bear market environment. The quantitative model for an oversold condition in a bull market may not give an accurate reading in a bear market.

The long-term behavior of a stock price depends on the company's financial results (earnings, cash flow, assets and liabilities, etc.). However, short-term and intermediate price trends are sometimes influenced by technical factors and "technical signals." Such signals can become a self-fulfilling prophecy for investors. For example, some investors believe that stocks will go down at certain times of the year. If a majority of investors expect September to be the worst month of the year, with a bottom taking place in october, then why would they bother to buy stocks in August? They would just wait, then buy stocks cheaper in late September or early October. When such "mechanical rules" become popular, most investors tend to follow them. They are, in effect, creating the technical pattern that they anticipate will take place.

Trading against the crowd and the emotions of fear and greed.

"Common stocks should be purchased when their prices are low, not after they have risen to high levels during an upward bull market. Buy, when everyone else is selling, and hold on until everyone else is buying – This is more than just a catchy slogan. It is the very essence of successful investment." J. Paul Getty

The crowd (the public) often has difficulties controlling the emotions of fear and greed. They get very pessimistic and nervous near a bottom and very optimistic and euphoric near a top.

Professional money managers take advantage of these situations as prices in the open market are below their intrinsic value.

When the American Association of Individual Investors (AAII) weekly survey shows an extreme level of bearishness (above 50%) and a low level of bullishness (near 25%) it usually precedes gains in the market. As the saying goes "it is always darkest before the dawn"

(VIX) The CBOE Volatility Index

The CBOE Volatility Index (VIX) is a measure of the level of implied volatility in index options. The VIX is intended to indicate the implied volatility of 30-day index options (eight OEX calls and puts). This volatility is constructed using the implied volatilities using a wide range of S&P 500 index options. (VIX) tends to increase near market bottoms. On August 16, 2007 the (VIX) hit a peak of 37.5 when the S&P500, the NASDAQ and the DJIA made a reversal from what looked like a bottomless pit to close unchanged for the day. It was a 6% U turn which was followed by a steep decline in the VIX to 33.7. Subsequently the (VIX) dropped to 19. A higher VIX indicates more nervousness in the market.

In September 2001 and in July 2002, near the market bottom, the volatility index reached a level of over 50, giving an extreme oversold reading and a buy signal. A high (VIX) is a sign of fear and capitulation in the options market. It takes place when investors buy put options to hedge stock portfolios or sell call options to earn income.

A higher VIX indicates more nervousness. When the VIX is high it often tends to remain high for several weeks which give you enough time to buy and you don't have to jump in the first reading of high VIX.

(VXN) CBOE NASDAQ – 100 Volatility Index

(VXN) is a key measure of market expectations of near term volatility conveyed by NASDAQ – 100 index (NDX) options prices. It measures the market's expectationsof 30-day volatility implicit in the prices of near-term NASDAQ -100 options

Moving averages

A moving average (also known as simple moving average) is calculated in a continuous manner. New data is added and the oldest data is subtracted each time the moving average is calculated. For example, a 50-day moving average of price data is calculated by adding the latest day price and subtracting the oldest day price and then divided by 50. It is always a 50-day average of the most recent 50 days. The reason for calculating a moving average is to smooth the day-to-day fluctuation in prices and to enable you to better identify a trend. Prior to making a final trading decision, you should look at both short-term, intermediate term and long-term trends. Many technical analysts use the 50-day moving average as support and resistance levels for short-term and intermediate-term trading.

Many professionals use the 200-day moving average as a tool in defining price trends and in identifying support and resistance levels. The 80 week moving average is considered a short-term bottom indicator (July 2006, August 2007). The moving averages are also used as an indication of the level of risk in the market. When the proportion of the NYSE stocks are trading above the 200-day moving average, this would be worrisome for the equity market. A moving average is often used as a trade trigger (to buy calls or buy puts) when prices crossover a moving average on the upside or the downside. Many traders use the 200 day moving average to trigger a sell signal when the price of several major market indexes such as the S&P 500, the Dow Jones Industrials and the Nasdaq 100 drop below their 200 day moving average.

Overbought / Oversold Market Conditions

An overbought market condition is a market near a top. An oversold market condition is a market near a bottom. Not all market bottoms and market tops have the same patterns, and not all timing indicators will give accurate timing signals all the time. Several indicators will give leading signals; other will give lagging signals. What you are facing is expected probabilities, which may help you to determine a buy range or sell range for short-term or long-term decisions. In addition to prices relative to moving averages, and other classical patterns such as head and shoulder formations, unusual volume activity is also very important. Volume activity near market bottom often increases as the public investor panic.

TRIN —The Short-Term Trading Index, also known as the ARMS Index

TRIN is the ratio of two other ratios. It is a ratio of the Issues ratio (I) divided by the Volume ratio (V). (I) is equal to the number of up issues divided by the number of down issues. (V) is equal to the volume in advancing issues divided by the volume in declining issues. TRIN = (I) / (V). (I) = Number of issues up / number of issues down.

(V) = Upside volume / downside volume. For example: In a day when the advancing issues are equal to 900 issues and the declining issues are also equal to 900 issues, the ratio of advancing issues to declining issues is equal to one. If the volume of advancing issues is equal to 600 million shares and the volume in declining issues are equal to 300 million shares, the ratio of up volume to down volume is equal to two. The resulting ratio of issues to volume is a TRIN equal to 0.50. The reading of 0.50 indicates that the daily volume on the NYSE is twice as strong as the number of issues traded on the day. The 10-day moving average of TRIN is used to identify oversold market condition (market bottom). When the 10-day TRIN reaches 1.50 the market is near an oversold condition giving a buy signal.

Technical timing statistics that gives good trend signals in a secular structural sustained bull market may not be functioning well and may require different level of signals in a secular structural sustained bear market. A reading of an oversold condition (10-day moving average of over 1.40) may give an accurate buy signal in a structural bull market but may not give an accurate reading in a bear market. A reading of an oversold condition (10-day moving average of over 1.60 rather than 1.40) may be required to identify an oversold condition in a bear market. Not only the level of oversold reading may be higher, the frequency pattern of the oversold signals is different. In a bear market, you can get many repeated oversold signals before you arrive at a true bottom.

A high TRIN of 10-day average above 1.50 together with simultaneously a 1-day reading of below 0.5 indicates buying into an oversold condition (market bottom). A 10-day average below 0.50 and a 1-day reading above 2.00 indicate selling into an overbought condition (market top). A 5-day moving average of below 0.40 is considered a signal for an overbought market condition.

Market Seasonality; September, October and the 4th Quarter

Historically, September and October have been challenging months. The crashes of 1929, 1987 and 1997 all took place during October. However, the market often hits bottom in October and then rallies in November and December (the so-called year-end rally). Since its inception in 1896, the DJIA during the month of September has shown an average loss of 1.1% (Wall St. Journal, Sunday 9/1/2002).

Average Gain or Loss for DJIA per Month (1896-2002)
(Source: Wall St. Journal)

Jan. +1.2%, Feb. -0.2%, March +0.7%, April +1.1%, May -0.1% June +0.4%
July +1.2% Aug +1.4% Sept. %-1.1 Oct . +0.2% Nov. +0.9% Dec. +1.2%

From 2000 to 2006 , the S&P 500 average return during October was 2.6% and the 4th quarter has been up six out of seven years with an average return of about 5.5% Since 1950, the S&P has returned 1.8% in November, 1.7% in December and 1.4% in January, according to the Stock Traders Almanac.

The January effect

The market generally rises during the month of January. Investors will buy during the last two weeks in December in anticipation of prices going up in January.

Presidential four-year election cycle

Political pressures during the four-year presidential cycle have affected the behavior of stock prices. During the first year after the presidential election, the stock market (the S&P 500) tends to rise only modestly. Then, the election is over and political pressures subside. In the second year of the four-year cycle, the market does slightly better than the first year. The third year is often the best year as the administration promises to use monetary and fiscal policies to stimulate the economy. During the fourth year, the administration usually paints a rosy economic picture in anticipation for the next election, but the risk of the unknown election results creates some uncertainty. The fourth year is usually better than the first and the second year but not as good as the third.

Mutual Funds, Cash Reserves as a Percentage of Their Assets

Cash reserves as a percentage of assets can vary from growth fund to growth and income fund to income equity funds. A low percentage of cash reserve (below 4%) is generally observed near market top. A relatively high percentage (over 8%) is observed near market bottom. This percentage will vary under bull market or bear market condition.

New lows for the year vs. new highs for the year

Timing indicators will help you to compare current market conditions to similar market behavior in the past. Near market bottom, investors tend to be pessimistic and selling activity rises. As a result, a large number of stocks hit new lows for the year. For example, in October 1987, when the market hit bottom, some 1,516 stocks reached a new low for the year. When the number of stocks hitting new highs is very few (10–15) and the number of stocks hitting new lows is very large (over 500), the market is probably near a bottom. The divergence between the number of issues that reach new highs and the number of issues making new lows also indicates that the conviction of investors in the market direction is weakening.

Market Breadth

Market breadth is positive when the number of issues advancing exceeds the number of issues declining. Market breadth is negative when the number of issues declining exceeds the number of issues advancing. This is especially significant when the market hits a new high but the market breadth is negative giving you a negative signal.

Price gaps

Gaps in price charts can be used as a timing tool. A gap in the price often indicates a change in trend, especially if it is accompanied by an increase in volume. Prices will tend to rise following an upgap and continue to decline after a down gap over an intermediate term. An illustration of a price gap is presented in Figure 5.3. On September 23, 2000, Intel dropped from 62 to 49, registering a down gap in the price formation and giving a bearish signal. From a price of 75 in July 2000, Intel dropped to 13 in October 2002.

Insiders' buying and selling activity, Insiders transaction ratio

Corporate insiders (officers and directors of public companies) who have access to insider information often buy and sell based on their in-depth knowledge of their company's outlook. When the overall activity of insiders' selling rises, it indicates that they are becoming more pessimistic and a market top is near. When insiders' buying activity rises, it indicates that stocks are cheap and the insiders are buying near market bottom. Insiders by regulation are required to disclose to the SEC their buying and selling activity. There are many legitimate reasons why insiders may buy and sell stocks. But when several insiders (3 or more) sell or buy large number of shares, this may indicate that some kind of important news — good or bad —is pending. When you see a large number of insiders selling in many companies, it indicates that many executives believe that stock prices are too high. This could indicate a market top. The Insiders Transaction Ratio is the ratio of insiders sells to insiders buys. A ratio over 20 to 1 is considered bearish. A ratio under 12 to 1 is considered bullish,

Public pessimism vs. public optimism — a contrarian view

Buy when everyone is selling, and sell when everyone is buying. It is an important rule to successful investing. Taking a contrarian view to public psychology can help you determine market top and bottom conditions. The American Association of Individual Investors gives statistics on percentage of individuals who are bullish. This is provided by Investors Intelligence (30 Church Street, PO Box 2046, New Rochelle, NY 10801). A high percentage of individual bulls (above 50%) is considered bearish by contrarian investors. A high percentage of bears (above 50%) is considered bullish by contrarian investors.

IPOs activity

IPO stands for Initial Public Offering. After a long period of public optimism, investors are often eager to buy a large number of new issues of initial public offerings. When the number of new issues accelerates to a point where almost every day another company goes public, or raises capital through a secondary offering, it usually indicates that a market top is near.

Issues advancing minus issues declining (also known as Breadth)

This indicator is also known as the breadth indicator which describes the action of the market. An index such as DIA (Dow Industrial Average) may be influenced by only a few stocks going up, while most stocks in the market may be declining, indicating underlying weakness in the market. The advance minus decline line is a cumulative calculation of the net difference of cumulative advances minus cumulative declines.

Investment Advisory Newsletters (bearish/bullish)

This indicator is surveyed by Investors Intelligence. It shows how many newsletters are bearish and how many are bullish. When a large number of newsletters are bearish and gloomy, reacting to stock market weakness and recommending moving into cash, this indicator gives a bullish contrarian signal and the market is usually near a bottom. When most advisory letters are bullish, the market is usually near a top.

NYSE Stocks above 200-day moving average and below 200-day moving average

When more than 70 percent of the NYSE stocks are above the 200-day moving average, it indicates over-optimism by the crowd and indicates an overbought market condition. This condition should be worrisome to the professional investor. When more than 70 percent of the NYSE stocks are below the 200-day moving average, it indicates over-pessimism by the crowd.. When the market turns upward following a decline of over 20% in the S&P 500, much of the return is achieved in the first year. The following shows that it is a good time to buy after the S&P has declined more than 20%.

During the period 1962-2000, the market fluctuated both up and down. If you bought the S&P 500 every time after the market declined more than 20%, your average annual return during the first three years would be as follows: After one year: 39.4%. After two years : 24.9%. After three years: 16.1%.

(Source: University of Chicago Center for Research in Securities Prices.)

Put/call ratio

The put/call ratio is the ratio of the daily volume of put to the daily volume of call options on the Standard & Poor 100. The ratio is a contrary indicator. High pessimism (large volume of puts) is viewed as bullish. High optimism (large volume of calls) is viewed as bearish. A ratio of over 2.0 indicates high pessimism. When put activity rises (one measure of pessimism), and when call activity drops, the market is probably near a bottom. When you compare the number of new puts to open to the number of new calls to open, an aggressive level of call buying has not boded well for stocks

Support resistance levels / accumulation distribution patterns

Academicians and professional portfolio managers have long debated the predictive value of chart formation. When you study the performance history of the market through charts, you distinguish between the company as an operational entity and the stock price movement trading on an exchange. In other words, the company and the performance of its stock are two different factors to consider. For example, IBM's revenues and profits may go up in a given time period, yet its stock price may decline. The professional trader is trying to identify the price range in which buyers will be attracted to buy (demand) and at what prices seller will be attracted to sell (supply). Chart formations indicate different buying and selling activities. For example, a "head and shoulder" price formation gives a sell signal when the price declines below the neckline of its right shoulder. A head-and-shoulder chart formation literally looks like a left shoulder, right shoulder and a head. A reverse head and shoulder formation indicates buying activity. A breakaway upside gap formation indicates buying activity and gives a good signal for a new upside move and new up trend. A breakaway downside gap indicates selling activity and gives a good signal for a new downtrend. Moving averages are often used as support an resistance levels. Significant changes in volume may indicate a bottom or a top formation.

Support, Resistance and options strike prices.

When you select strike prices for calls and puts trading, you may use technical resistance levels to determine the strike price for selling or buying "out of the money calls and you can use technical support levels to determine the strike price for selling or buying "out of the money" puts. These technical tools can be used in addition to standard deviation and volatility calculations.

Volume: the Weapon of the Bull

You need unusual good volume for a good rally to be sustained. A low volume rally after an oversold market condition is a bearish signal and can be used as an opportunity to sell into the rally.

Short Interest

Short Interest can be used as an indicator for the longer-term direction of the market. Short interest is the total number of shares of a stock that were sold short by investors and are still "open" (not been covered yet or "closed"). The investors who sold short expect the stock to fall. It describes the market sentiment relative to a particular stock or a particular sector. An increase in short interest may help you in evaluate your risk of buying or holding the stock or the opportunity or profit potential of buying put options. Instead of shorting a stock you can buy a put option on the stock. Buying a put option (a bearish bet) involves much less risk than shorting a stock and reduces the cost of the transaction. The NYSE short-interest ratio calculates the monthly short interest on the entire exchange divided by the average daily volume of the NYSE for the last month. Contrarian investors use the short interest data as a tool to evaluate the overall level of pessimism. A very high short interest over an extended period of time tells you that the "bad news" is probably already reflected in the price of the stock and it is time to be bullish. Short sellers will have to buy the stock to cover their shorts as they have to return the borrowed shares to the lender.

Combination of Timing Indicators

Timing indicators do not give accurate signals all the time. Their reliability will vary from one market to another (bull or bear markets). As an investor, you should not arrive at a decision based on a reading of one indicator. Rather, you should use a combination or a composite of several indicators. For example in identifying a major market bottom you want to see a high 10-day average TRIN (above 1.50), a high Volatility Index -VIX (above 50), a relatively high level of mutual funds cash position (above 5%), a high level of investor advisors bearish (over 50%), a high percentage of stock below 200-day moving average (above 70%), a large number of stocks reaching new lows for the year (above 500) and pessimistic comments on front pages of magazines. Different markets can reach different levels of oversold condition (a market bottom and a buy range). You should try to get an overall picture of the point in time in the market cycle.

Timing vs. Value analysis

Over the years, value analysis, which is based on the analysis of balance sheet income statements, and the corporate business model, has proven to be the key to long-term investment success. (Point in case: Warren Buffet is known for his use of value analysis.) Timing has been a more significant tool for short-term trading.

Do stocks or ETFs always come back?

Many investors, when facing losses, will say, "I'm not worried; the market always comes back." What's wrong with this kind of thinking is that indexes, such as the DJIA or S&P500, always do come back, but individual stocks, such as Bethlehem Steel, Lucent, and Polaroid —often do NOT come back. Or, it may take many years for the stocks to come back to their old highs. This is why investing in ETFs is a superior strategy for the small investors. ETFs as an index tracking vehicle offer the security of the market "coming back" without the risk of individual stock volatility.

Is It a Market of Stocks or a Market of ETFs?

When an investor tells you that the market is oversold or near a bottom, which market is he referring to? There are many sectors, and there are many markets. The market may be oversold in one sector but overbought in another. Investing in ETFs involves investing in different markets rather than investing in different stocks.

The Trend Is Your Friend

A downtrend is marked by lower highs and lower lows. An uptrend is marked by higher highs and higher lows. You should distinguish between the value of the actual operating company and the price behavior of the stock in the open market. When you buy 100% of a company (in the case of a takeover), an in-depth fundamental analysis is required. When you buy shares in the open market, identifying the price trend is more relevant. The potential capital gain requires you to be sensitive to the price behavior of a stock. Buying into a good company that is in a downtrend will generate losses. Being long in an uptrend and short in a downtrend is the key to success in short-term trading.

When the number of stocks hitting new lows is very large (over 500), the market is probably near a bottom. A change in trend is a change in opportunities. Every investor is attempting to buy stocks that go up and sell stocks that go down. Unfortunately, that's easier said than done!

"Don't try to buy at the bottom and sell at the top. This can't be done except by liars."
Bernard M. Baruch

CHAPTER 8

EVALUATING PERFORMANCE

The portfolio manager's "added value" (ALPHA).

The manager's "added value" is measured by (ALPHA). The manager's ALPHA is equal to the excess return over a predetermined benchmark. The benchmark could be the performance of the Russell 3000 or the 10 year yield on treasuries. The level of (ALPHA) depends on the manager's ability to select the ETFs (or the underlying securities) that are deemed attractive to be included in the portfolio. It is also a function of the different correlations and the level of diversification of the portfolio's holdings. The investment decisions is often based both on "fundamental " analysis including dividends yields and P/E ratios. It also involves the calculations of statistical correlation and market timing analysis.

The benchmark for (ALPHA) calculations might be the CBOE "buy-write" index or the CBOE "Put" index which has generated an average of 12.6.% annual return. The Manager's "ALPHA " annual return is equal to any excess return beyond the 12.6%.The portfolio manager "added value" is in the selection of the ETFs (the underlying securities) that are deemed attractive to be included in the portfolio. Determining the period of time used to calculate beta (one year or 6 months). The selection of ETFs with different correlations and developing the risk management models (based on fundamental analysis of asset classes including dividends yields and P/E ratios), will enhance the "alpha" return. The managers "value added" is any excess return beyond 12.6%

and at the same time the reduction in the downside volatility risk.

Past performance of the "CBOE S&P 500 put write" index.

The Chicago board options exchange has back tested data covering the last 20 years showing that the "sell put" strategy produced an annual return of 12.6% with lower volatility than a "buy write" strategy and with lower volatility than the underlying index (S&P500). The selling puts strategy involves the selling of one month at the money options on the S&P500 as a single ETF underlying security.

Past performance of the "CBOE S& P500 BuyWrite" Index

A "buy-write" monthly index (BXM) index is a "covered call" index. Each month, a new S&P 500 near-term call, at-the-money is sold. The call will have approximately one month left to expiration. The call has an exercise price just above the prevailing index level (i.e. slightly out-of-the-money). The premium collected is added to the portfolio's total value. The SPX call is held until expiration, at which time a new one-month call is written, The expired call, if exercised, is settled for cash. Data available from 01-03-2005 to 05-01-07 indicates an average annual return of 9.3% for the Buy-Write monthly index. Several mutual funds using a covered writing strategy have produced an average annual return of about a 10%. Furthermore, the beta of the covered writing portfolios was near 0.50, suggesting that the volatility of the covered call writing portfolios was about half of the volatility of the S&P500 volatility. The "Buy-Write" index is similar to the "Sell Put" index. There are over 30 publicly traded mutual funds that use covered writing strategies: For example: (BEP) CBOE S&P500 covered calls closed-end fund currently selling at a premium to NAV of 9% and paying a dividend of

10%. Since its inception on 03-15-05, it generated an average annual return of 8.14%. The investment strategy is simple: Buy the S&P500 and sell call options. The fund beta is 0.43, and it management fee is 1.07%

The Eaton Vance group of funds has 5 option income funds; (EOI) Enhanced equity income. Its inception date was 10-29-04. It invests in large and mid-cap stocks and sell call option on a portion of the securities. Average annual return since inception is 12.2%. (EOS) Enhance equity income II is similar to EOI. (ETB) Eaton Vance Tax-Managed BuyWrite income fund; inception date 04-27-2005. It has generated so far an average annual performance of 12%. It owns a diversified portfolio of common stocks and sells the S&P500 call options. The fund beta is 0.48 and the management fee is 1.10%. (ETW) Eaton Vance Tax-Managed Global Buy-write opportunities. The inception date was 09-30-05. The current distribution is 9%. The average annual return is 9.46%.

Past performance of the dynamic ETFs
Equity income Core / Satellite strategy

All in all. there are over 500 ETFs today. Among these are included domestic ETFs for almost every sector and industry. There are ETFs for most broad based indexes, total market indexes, large cap indexes, mid and small cap. indexes. There are many international and regional ETFs. Most ETFs are relatively new and little historical performance data is available given their "short life" to date. However, performance data is available for the CBOE BuyWrite monthly index (BXM). In this BuyWrite index each month a new near-term call, at-the-money S&P500 index (SPX) (it will have approximately one month left to expiration) is sold, with an exercise price just above the prevailing index level (i.e. slightly out of the money). The premium collected is added to the portfolio's total value. The SPX call is held until expiration, at which time a new one-month call is written. The expired call, if exercised, is settled for cash. Data extending over the range from 01-03-2005 to 05-01-07 indicates an average annual return of 9.3% for the BuyWrite monthly index. Several mutual funds using a covered writing strategy have produced an average annual return of about a 10%. Furthermore, the beta of the covered writing portfolios was near 0.50 suggesting that the volatility of the covered call writing portfolios was about ½ of the volatility of the S&P500 volatility. We believe that using a mix of ETFs instead of only one index (such as the S&P500), and through diversification and prevention of excessive correlation, the average annual rate of return can be increased and the downside volatility risk can be reduced. When no leverage is used, the portfolio is expected to produce a net annual return of 12%-14% (after fees and expenses). With the use of leverage, the expected rate of return could reach 18%-20%.

The Sharp Ratio

In 1966 the Sharpe ratio was introduced as a measure for the performance of mutual funds. The Sharp Ratio is a measure of risk-adjusted return of an investment. It compares the "risk-free" return (For example – 3 month treasury bills) to the actual return for an investment over a period of time (a month, a year). You calculate the "excess return" over the "risk-free" return. This return is what you "earned" for assuming some "risk". Risk is measured by the standard deviation of the returns. The Sharpe ratio is equal to: Excess return divided by the standard deviation of the returns . A Sharpe ratio of over 1.0 indicates good performance. Performance measures usually are based on historical data. The assumption often is that future performance is somewhat correlated to historical performance and therefore has some predictive ability. The Sharpe Ratio is dependent on the time period that it measures. (For example one year.)

Annualized Standard Deviation

The statistical measurement of risks and returns is a dynamic process. The correlation between to ETFs is often calculated on a six-month, one-year or three-years period. The standard deviation is often presented as an average over a period of time and does not reveal the one week or one-month declines in N.A.V.. The annualized standard deviation can be used as a relative measurement of performance of two or more investment portfolios.

Know your Beta

Beta is a statistical measure of stock volatility in relation to market volatility. The S&P500 has a beta coefficient of 1. A beta below 1 indicates that the stock is more stable than the S&P 500. It is important to know the beta of each holding in your portfolio. If you expect an economic recession you should invest in low beta stocks.

Look for changes in Beta

A change in beta (up or down) may signal a change in relative strength or a change in trend. Knowing the beta of your stocks is very important as it helps you to know and control your risks.

Mixed Correlations

Correlation is a statistical measure of the degree to which the movements of two variables (stock/ETF) are related. Results range from -1.0 to + 1.0. The correlation between two or more ETFs is critical in managing and mitigating risks since you do not want your portfolio to be a one directional portfolio. Namely, you do not want all your positions to move in the same direction during a period of market declines. Some of your portfolio's holdings should go up when other holdings decline.

Performance during a period of market decline.

It is important to reduce the risk of losses during periods of a market decline. This objective is achieved by employing an investment strategy that involves primarily selling put options on ETFs, selling call options on ETFs, and investing in a diversified portfolio of ETFs (Exchange Traded Funds). This includes several "short ETFs" known as "Bear Market" ETFs. A quantitative approach helps in execution of a defensive strategy. Quantitative analysis does not depend on the investment skills of a portfolio manager to pick the right stock or the right sector. .

The performance during an unexpected "event driven" market drop

Historically an "event-driven" market decline of over 10% is expected on the average to take place in about 1 out of 16 – 18 months. Since low beta ETFs together with a low correlation of ETFs are used, the result is a low level of concentration of exposures. The portfolio's decline is expected to be at a much lower percentage than the overall market. The portfolio performance is also a function of the time frame (duration) of the decline and the subsequent bounce back reversal that follows. Since performance is usually reported on a monthly basis and since most reversals to the upside take place within a month, the effect on monthly performance is expected to be relatively small.

During a prolonged bear market, several written put options will be assigned as you are obligated to buy the underlying securities. In that case covered call options will be written. During that time the portfolio will be:(A) Short "out of the money" puts.

(B) Long underlying ETFs

(C) Short "in the money" calls.

In cases when the open-market prices are below intrinsic value (ETFs are undervalued) you can advantage of market opportunities and buy the underlying undervalued securities and then sell covered calls into a market strength.

The selection of a diversified portfolio of equity ETFs, fixed income ETFs, commodities, currencies or other ETFs together with securities with different beta and low or negative correlation will prevent the portfolio's holdings from all moving at the same direction at the same time and will substantially reduce the probability that the portfolio's N.A.V will decline in value when the market (S&P500 for example) declines.

Open Interest and Average daily volume of options trading.

Several ETFs options are thinly traded or do not have listed options. It is therefore important that you select primarily ETFs with actively traded options. Lack of volume will have a negative effect on the ability to execute trades and could have a negative impact on performance.

Gains from Selling Put and Call options

In addition to diversification with different correlations by asset classes, by sectors, indexes and global investing, selling (short) put and call options also reduces the portfolio's volatility. During periods of market declines gains from selling call options reduces some of the losses from selling put options. During periods of rising markets gains from selling puts reduces the losses on short calls.

Managing risk during a prolonged period of a bear market

During a prolonged period of a bear market the put options to be sold should be "out-of-the-money" to reduce the downside risk exposure. The call options to be sold should be "in-the-money". You should invest in "Bear Market" and UltraShort ETFs that go up in value when the overall market declines. See list of Bear Market and UltraShort ETFs in chapter 9.

Relative Performance

Past performance does not guarantee future results. Investment returns and principal value of portfolios will vary with market conditions and are subject to various risks. . Many portfolio managers, including university professors, will admit that it is difficult to outperform the stock market consistently over time. The subject of relative performance has been a matter of continuing debate both among professional and the investment public. Statistically it is very difficult to prove that active portfolio managers outperform due to their skill and not luck. According to S&P data, most active managers and stock pickers trail their benchmark indexes. For the five years, 1999-2003, mid-cap managers trailed the S&P Mid-Cap 400 by 7.36% per year. In the small-cap asset class, actively managed funds trailed the S&P by 4.65% per year. The large-cap actively managed funds performed almost equal to S&P500 as they delivered 99.76% of the index performance. On a cumulative basis the difference between Index and Sector investing and Stock picking rate of return could be substantial.

Do active managers add value in term of beating the performance of a specific index? The Vanguard 500 Index fund over 10 and 15 years has performed better than the average actively managed fund by about 2 percentage points a year. Actively managed funds have higher total expenses due to higher trading costs and higher administrative expenses.

The performance of managed portfolios is also a function of the manager's ability to execute a specific strategy. Individually managed accounts which offer more personalized service may nonetheless face difficulties such as the ability to achieve a specific level of diversification and liquidity. Investing in ETFs helps individually managed accounts achieve a higher level of diversification with higher liquidity and lower expenses and more flexibility of execution than investing in more actively managed alternatives.

Sector fund managers have argued that the probability of being right on an industry is higher than that of being right on an individual stock. In the case of individually managed portfolios, the portfolio's performance should be evaluated by the progress against the individual investor's financial objectives. An individual investor should evaluate portfolio performance relative to a market based performance rather than absolute performance. An investor who is down 5% when the S&P 500 is down 30% is doing relatively well. An investor who is up 5% when the S&P 500 is up 30% is doing poorly. Balanced portfolios should also be compared to the performance of the broad market. Performance research suggests that median active mutual fund managers have underperformed their passive benchmarks during 70% of the past 20 years.(Investment Guide for Plan Sponsors, "Why Most Active Managers Underperform," Robert C. Jones, Institutional Investor, July 30, 1998). The comparative performance of index-linked funds helps confirm the benefits of a low-cost, low-turnover, diversified investment strategy.

Stock performance vs. Bond performance.

The return comparison between stocks (exemplified by the S&P 500) and bonds shows that the S&P 500 percentage return was higher than the return from fixed income securities (corporate bonds and treasuries), excluding the period of July 2000 to June 2002.

TABLE 8A
Comparison of Returns between Stocks and Bonds through June 2002

Returns from:	S&P 500 Stocks	Intermediate Bonds	Treasury Bills
July 2000	-16.4%	9.5%	3.9%
Dec. 1995	9.2	6.4	4.7
Dec. 1990	12.4	7.5	4.5

Dec. 1985	12.6	8.0	5.2
Dec. 1980	13.1	9.8	6.4
Dec. 1975	13.3	8.9	6.6
Dec. 1970	11.6	8.5	6.5
Dec. 1960	10.8	7.4	6.0
Dec. 1950	11.8	6.4	5.2

Do active managers add value in term of beating the performance of a specific index? The Vanguard 500 over 10 and 15 years has performed better than the average actively managed fund by about 2 percentage points a year. Actively managed funds have higher total expenses due to higher trading costs and higher administrative expenses.

The performance of managed portfolios is also a function of the manager's ability to execute a specific strategy. Individually managed accounts which offer more personalized service may face difficulties such as the ability to achieve a specific level of diversification and liquidity. Investing in ETFs helps individually managed accounts achieve a higher level of diversification with higher liquidity and lower expenses and more flexibility of execution. Using a mix of ETFs instead of only one index (such as the S&P500) and through diversification and correlation analysis, the average annual rate of return can be increased and the downside volatility risk can be reduced.

TAX CONSIDERATIONS

"It is not what you make. It is what you keep."

Tax considerations can significantly affect the gains or losses when buying or selling ETFs and or options. Your tax advisor should be consulted. The information and conclusions provided in this chapter are only for general information of tax regulations and may not be applicable to every individual investor or any specific tax case. See the prospectuses of ETFs for more complete tax information. Tax laws are subject to change. Investors are advised to consult with their tax specialist to evaluate the tax consequences of any personal investment strategy. Certain option strategies are not suitable for every investor. This chapter summarizes some of the federal income tax rules for individual U. S. citizens and U. S. residents who are engaged in taxable transactions. Corporation and tax-exempt organizations may be subject to different tax laws.

Taxes on Exchange-Traded Fund Shares

When you invest in an ETF you pay most capital gains taxes at the final sale of the fund. While you own the ETF you can invest the money that would have been paid for taxes until the final sale of the fund.

ETFs have several possible legal structures. They include open-end funds, unit investment trusts known as UITs, Grantor trusts, Exchange traded notes (ETNs) and Master Limited Partnerships (MLPs). The gains and dividend income of these ETFs may be taxed differently from each other. In the case partnerships the partners receive form K-1 for the annual tax reports..

With traditional mutual funds, returns are reduced by expenses, management fees and by taxes on capital gains distribution. There are more than 8000 actively managed funds available to investors, but many fail to perform closely to their benchmark. It is difficult to beat the benchmark index.

For federal income taxs, ETFs shares are generally taxed as interest in a mutual fund. Dividends paid from investment income, including interest and net shot-term capital gains, are taxable as ordinary income, whether you take them in cash or reinvest them in a fund. "Qualified Dividends" are taxed at the qualified dividends tax rate. Capital gains distribution from long-term capital gains are taxable as long-term capital gains regardless of the length of time an investor has owned the fund's shares.

Taxes on iPath ETNs

The sale, redemption or maturity of ETNs will generate tax consequences, in certain cases, you may be required to make a specific election in order to receive the most favorable tax treatment. Investing in ETNs is not equivalent to direct investing in an index or index components. The investor fee will reduce the amount of your return at maturity or on redemption, and as a result you may receive less than the principal amountof your investments at maturity or upon redemption of your securities even if the value of the relevant index has increased.

Capital Gains and Losses

After July 1, 2001, the Economic Growth and Tax Relief Reconciliation Act of 2001 (the 2001 Act) reduced the top marginal tax rate from 39.6% to 35%, phased in over a five-year period.

The long-term capital gain rate is generally taxed at a maximum rate of 15% for taxable years beginning before Jan.1, 2011. The maximum rate of long-term capital gains will return to 20% in 2011.

Distribution in excess of a fund's current and accumulated earnings and profits are treated as a tax-free return of capital to the extent of your basis in the shares, and as capital gains thereafter.

Generally speaking, "sell" decisions should be based on the merit of each investment rather than on the desire to achieve a lower tax rate, by waiting for an extended period of time to reach the 12 months' date. Waiting could result in investment losses that exceed the tax savings. Another item to consider is the Alternative Minimum Tax.

Short-Sale Rules

The short-sale tax rules deal with situations in which an investor holds or at a later date acquires a "substantially identical property." Each specific case should be discussed with your accountant. Special attention should be given to cases of "in the money" options.

Long Stock and Long Calls

If a stock or a call is held for more than a year, the gain or the loss is a long-term gain or loss. If the stock or the long call is sold in less than a year, the tax loss or gain is short-term. Expiration of an option is treated as a sale (long-term or short-term. Upon exercise of a call, the tax cost of the underlying security includes the premium paid for the option, including commission.

Short Calls

If the short option expires, the premium received is always a short-term premium. If the option is exercised and the underlying security is sold, the selling price of the underlying security for tax purposes includes the premium received from the sale of the call. The premium received is not considered income if distributed on the day the short call was opened.

Wash-Sale Rule

The Wash-Sale rule does not allow investors to reacquire "substantial identical" securities within a 30-day period before or after selling securities at a loss. The loss could be disallowed if within the 30 days the investor sells an in-the-money put. This should also be discussed with your accountant.

Tax Treatment of International Securities

If you are a U.S. citizen, you will incur the same capital gains, divided and interest taxes from international securities as you would from U.S. securities. Many countries withhold taxes on dividend income paid to shareholders from other countries. By filing a foreign tax credit on your tax return you may recover the amount withheld. For iShares of international (foreign) countries, there is no additional foreign tax on the dividends, as you would pay on any common stock.

Year-End Tax-Loss Planning and Strategies

"Nothing is certain but death and taxes", but you can use ETFs to implement year-end tax strategies. You can not eliminate taxes but you can minimize their impact. You can maintain your asset allocation, using ETFs with high correlation. You can sell a stock to realize a tax loss and replace it with an investment in an ETF with a high correlation or in a similar sector with similar investment objectives. You can keep your ETF position for 30 days to avoid a wash-sale rule. This strategy of swapping individual stocks for similar sector ETFs will help the investor keep an industry sector exposure during the waiting period. This is important especially when the industry bounces back. The following is an example of several large-cap stocks for possible swapping with similar sector based ETFs.

Stock Symbol	Stock Name	ETF Symbol	ETF Name
AMGN	Amgen	IBB	Biotechnology NASDAQ
		BBH	Biotech HOLDRS trust
XOM	Exxon Mobil	IYE	Dow Jones U.S. Energy Sector
		XLE	Energy Select Sector SPDR
GE	General Electric	IYJ	Dow Jones U.S. Industrial Sector
		DIA	Diamonds Dow Jones Industrials
PFE	Pfizer	IYH	Healthcare Dow Jones sector index
		XLV	Healthcare Select Sector
		PPH	Pharmaceutical HOLDRS trust

Tax-loss strategies are often used in high volatility sectors such as technology. You can switch and swap among similar ETFs. For example:

Symbol	ETF Name	Symbol	ETF Swapp Name
QQQ	NASDAQ 100	XLK	Technology – Select Sector SPDR
		IYW	Dow Jones U.S. Technology Sector
MDY	Mid-Cap S&P 400 Trust	IJK	Mid-Cap 400 Growth Index iShares
		IWP	Russell Mid-Cap Growth iShares

The past correlation of performance between stock prices and ETF prices could change in the future because of possible changes in ETF holdings and changes in the price behavior of specific stocks relative to the price behavior of specific indexes. The most recent prices can be obtained from different sources. Switching expenses and charges, liquidity and volume information and ETF prospectuses can be obtained from your broker. You should avoid buying shares in funds that are going to make a year-end distribution before ex-dividend date.

Options trading for year-end tax planning

The objective is to transfer short term losses from one year to the next using calendar spreads. A calendar spread is the simultaneous purchase and sale of options in the underlying stock, with the same exercise price but with different expiration dates. If successful, for example these "rollover" transactions will be closed so that a short term loss is created in the current year (2007), and a short term gain is created during next year (2008).

Tax Risk

Although several funds seek to minimize and defer the federal income taxes incurred by common shareholders, there can be no assurance that they will be successful in this regard. The tax treatment of those funds distributions may change over time due to changes in the mix of investment returns and changes in the Federal tax laws. The provisions of the code applicable to qualified dividend income are set to expire at the close of 2010.

After Tax Performance Measurement

For portfolios subject to taxes (non-IRA or retirement accounts), a more accurate measure of performance is after-tax rate of return. The following is a summary of some basic rules related to federal income tax for individuals who are citizens or residents of the United States, and who are subject to taxes when selling an investment.

Currently, any capital gain or loss realized upon a sale of shares is generally treated as long-term capital gain or loss if the shares have been held for more than one year and as short-term capital gain or loss if the shares have been held for one year or less. The ability to deduct capital losses may be limited.

PAST PERFORMANCE IS NO GUARANTEE OF FUTURE RESULTS

CHAPTER 9

DESCRIPTION AND PROFILES OF POPULAR ETFs

The following are the profiles of several selected widely held Exchange Traded Funds (ETFs) as of 01/18/08

(The Assets values, beta, Correlation, Dividend yield and P/E are continuously changing)

Fund Name	Ticker	Assets	Beta	Corre lation	Div. Yield	P/E
		Billions	.			
SPDR Trust S&P500	SPY	98.2	1.00	1.00	1.84%	15.8
iShares MSCI EAFE	EFA	51.9	1.06	0.86	2.53%	13.9
iShares MSCI Emerg. Mkts	EEM	28.9	1.73	0.47	1.28%	15.8
iShares TR S&P 500	IVV	17.9	1.00	1.00	1.90%	14.3
Powrsh. QQQ Nasdaq 100	QQQQ	21.8	1.20	0.62	0.28%	26.3
iSha. Russell 1000 Growth	IWF	15.6	0 .98	0.83	0.91%	16.8
iSha Russell 2000 small-cap	IWM	11.2	1.35	0.77	1.02%	15.9
iShares MSCI Japan Fund	EWJ	10.1	1.01	0.35	1.04%	16.2

SPDR Mid-cap 400	MDY	10.1	1.16	0.95	1.17%	15.5
Vanguard Total Stock Mkt	VTI	10.3	1.02	1.00	1.79%	16.0
iSha Russell 1000 Value	IWD	10.5	1.02	0.82	2.40%	12.3
Diamond Series Trust 1	DIA	8.6	0.99	0.92	2.08%	15.7
iSha XINHAU China 25	FXI	7.2	1.45	0.35	1.20%	21.7
iSha Lehman 1-3 yr Treas.	SHY	9.5	(-0.04)	(-0.26)	4.27%	N/A
iSha MSCI Brazil	EWZ	7.6	2.11	0.36	1.48%	3.7
iSha Leh.U.S. aggr. bond	AGG	7.7	(-0.06)	(-0.52)	4.87%	N/A
Select Sec SPDR Energy	XLE	7.0	1.24	0.50	0.99%	12.4
iSha D. J. Select Dividend	DVY	6.9	0.97	0.48	3.66%	12.5
iSha S&P 500 growth	IVW	6.6	0.94	0.89	1.16%	15.7
Vanguard Emerging mkts k	VWO	6.0	1.59	0.45	1.88%	15.7
iSha Lehman TIPS bonds	TIP	5.3	(-0.12)	(-0.33)	4.14%	N/A
Financial Select S. SPDR	XLF	5.1	1.17	0.38	4.07%	11.9
iSha S&P Mid-Cap 400	IJH	4.9	1.17	0.95	1.29%	14.1
iShares S&P 100 Index	OEF	4.9	0.93	0.96	1.91%	14.1
iSha S&P small-cap 600	IJR	4.8	1.29	0.82	1.06%	15.1

iShares S&P 500 Value	IVE	4.5	1.05	0.91	2.31%	13.0
iSha MSCI Pacific ex Japan	EPP	4.1	1.17	0.60	4.68%	16.3
iSha Russell 2000 Value	IWN	4.0	1.31	0.44	2.03%	13.6
iShares Russell Mid-cap	IWR	3.9	1.10	0.91	1.37%	15.0
iShares Russell 1000	IWB	3.8	1.00	1.00	1.67%	14.3
iSha MSCI South Korea	EWY	3.7	1.61	0.60	0.57%	13.6
Oil Service Holders TR.	OIH	3.6	1.25	0.57	0.46%	11.8
iSha Russell 2000 Gowth	IWO	3.5	1.41	0.95	0.59%	18.8
Vanguard Growth ETF	VUG	3.2	0.9	0.79	0.93%	18.8
iSha Russel Mid-cap Grow	IWP	3.2	1.15	0.96	0.63%	16.1
iSh Invest. Grade cor. bonds	LQD	3.2	(-0.02)	-(0.44)	5.47%	N/A
iSha Russell Mid-cap Value	IWS	3.1	1.06	0.61	2.29%	13.7
iSharesLatin America 40	ILF	3.1	1.93	0.49	1.39%	15.2
Vanguard Eurpean	VGK	3.1	1.08	0.83	3.15%	13.2
iSha RUS 3000 Index Fd.	IWV	3.1	1.03	0.99	1.78%	14.4
Select Sector SPDR Techn.	XLK	3.0	1.11	0.74	0.72%	19.6

iSha Europe Mone. Union	EZU	2.9	1.13	0.72	2.47%	13.0
iShares S&P Europe 350	IEV	2.9	1.09	0.83	2.72%	12.9
iShares MSCI Taiwan	EWT	2.7	1.26	0.67	2.57%	13.2
Select Sector SPDR Util	XLU	2.5	0.77	0.29	2.57%	17.8
iSh Cohen&Steers Realty	ICF	2.1	1.24	0.07	4.06%	29.6
Pharmaceutical Holders	PPH	2.0	0.69	0.65	2.74%	14.7

Since an ETF is as good as the underlying securities in its portfolio it is important to know its objectives and the list of its portfolio holdings.

(SPY) STANDARD & POORS DEPOSITARY RECEIPTS (SPDR)

Trust Series 1 S&P 500
Category: Large Blend

SPDR Trust seeks to correspond to the price and yield performance, before fees and expenses, of the S&P 500 Index. SPDR trust is an exchange-traded fund that holds all of the S&P 500 index stocks. The S&P 500 is designed to be an indicator of U.S. equities. It reflects the risk/return characteristics of the large-cap universe. SPDRs trade on the AMEX. SPDRs are based on a broad market index. SPY is the oldest and largest ETF. SPY is an excellent alternative to S&P index funds, such as the Vanguard 500 Index. SPY has active listed options.

The top 5 holdings as of 08/31/07
(%) of the Fund

Exxon Mobil	3.69
General Electric	3.05
AT&T	1.87
Microsoft	1.85
Citicorp.	1.77

(EFA) ISHARES TR MSCI EAFE INDEX FD (NYSE)

Category: Foreign Large Blend.

EFA is one of the most popular ETFs. It is the second largest ETF. On Oct. 11. 2007 the N.A.V. reached $48.9 Bil. EFA gives the investor a significant international exposure. EFA seeks investment results that correspond generally to the price and yield performance, before fees and expenses, of the MSCI EAFE index. This index measures the performance of equities in developed European, Australian and Far East markets.

This fund contains 830 companies.

The top 5 holdings as of 08-31-07
(%) of the Fund

BP PLC	1.63
HSBC	1.52
Total SA	1.23
Toyota	1.20
Vodafone	1.15

(EEM) iShares MSCI Emerging MKTS Index Fund

Category: Mid-cap blend

Acts as a non-diversified fund, seeking investment results that correspond generally to the price and yield performance, before fees and expenses, of the MSCI Emerging Markets Index.

The top 5 holdings as of 08/31/07
(%) of the Fund

POSCO – ADR   4.12
Samsung Elect. GDR Regs 3.68
OAO Gasprom – ADR   3.61
Taiwan Semicon. – ADR   2.79
KOOKMIN Bank – ADR   2.34

(QQQQ) NASDAQ 100 TRUST SER 1

QQQQ tracks the price and yield performance of the NASDAQ 100 Index. Its portfolio includes all the stocks in the Nasdaq 100 Index, and was created to provide investors with the opportunity to purchase units of beneficial interest representing proportionate undevided interest in the portfolio. QQQQ is tech-rich.

Trading in QQQQ (formerly known as QQQ) was introduced by the AMEX in 1999. It is a unit investment trust designed to closely track the price and yield performance of the NASDAQ 100 index. It is a single security that holds all of the stocks in the NASDAQ 100 index. The QQQQ is an index fund that trades like a stock. You can buy and sell it any time, use limit orders and stop-loss orders. It trades on the AMEX under the symbol QQQQ. It measures the average performance of a broadly diversified group of stocks traded on the NASDAQ stock market. It includes the stocks of 100 of the largest and most actively traded nonfinancial companies listed on the NASDAQ stock market. The QQQQ is only part of the NASDAQ index (^IXIC), which is a broader index.

The top 5 holdings of the QQQQ (as of 06/30/07
(%) of the Fund

Apple   7.58
Costco   6.52
Google   5.42
Infosys   5.26
Microsoft   5.13

(IVV) iShares S&P 500 Index Fund.

Category: large-cap blend

(IVV) Operates as a non-diversified investment fund that seeks investment results that correspond to the performance of large-cap stocks as represented by the S&P 500 index.
The top 5 holdings are the same as (SPY)

(IWF) iShares Russell 1000 growth

Category: Large growth

Seeks investments returns that correspond to the performance of U.S. Large-cap growth stocks with the highest price-to-book ratios and forecasted growth within the Russell 1000, as represented by the Russell 1000 growth Index.
The top 5 holdings as of 08/31/07

	(%) of the fund' assets
Microsoft	3.08
Cisco	2.53
Intel	1.95
Hewlett- Packard	1.72
I.B.M.	1.66

(IWM) The Russell 2000 I Shares

Category: Small blend

The Russell 2000 index fund seeks investment results that correspond to the performance of publicly traded U.S. small-cap stocks, as represented by the Russell 2000 index. The index represents the 2000 smallest companies in the Russell 3000 index.
The top 5 holdings as of 08/31/07

	(%) of the Fund's assets
Exterran Holdings	0.34
CF Industries	0.26
FLIR Systems	0.24

| Chipotle Mexican | 0.23 |
| Priceline | 0.23 |

(EWJ) iShares MSCI JAPAN

Category: Japan Stock

Seeks to provide investment results that correspond generally to the price and yield performance of publicly traded securities in the aggregate in the Japanese market, as measured by the MSCI Japan Index.

The top 5 holdings as of 08/31/07

(%) of the Fund's assets

Toyota	5.52
Mitsubishi Fin.	2.72
Mizuho Fin.	2.10
Canon	2.10
Takeda Phrma.	2.02

(MDY) Mid-Cap Spiders

Category: Mid-Cap Blend

MDY started trading on the AMEX in 1995. The S&P Mid-Cap 400 ETF is one of more than 100 different exchange-traded funds listed on the American Stock Exchange. MDY tracks the S&P Mid-Cap 400 Index. It is a broadly diversified index representing a segment of the U.S. market of mid-sized companies. MDY represents ownership in the Mid-Cap SPDR trust, a long-term unit investment trust established to accumulate and hold a portfolio of common stocks. This portfolio is intended to provide investment results that generally correspond to the price performance and dividend yield of the S&P Mid-cap 400 Index. It is designed to provide a security whose market value approximates one fifth the value of the underlying S&P 400 Index.

Its attractiveness is in the fact that these mid-sized companies provide many opportunities for growth and have already developed beyond the uncertainties of small startup companies. The component stocks in this index include industries such as banks, chemicals, computers, and electric utilities. It is a market value weighted index in which each company's influence on the index is directly proportional to its market value. To find the portfolio's holdings of MDY, go to yahoo finance MDY and go to holdings. The top 5 holdings as 09/30/07

(%) of the Fund's assets

Intuitive Surg.	1.02
Cameron Int'l	0.88
Gamestop	0.78
Southwestern energy	0.73
Harris	0.69

(IWD) iShares Russell 1000 Value

Category: Large value

IWD seeks investment results that correspond to the performance of the U.S. large-cap value stocks with the lowest price to book ratios and forecasted growth within the Russell 1000, as represented by the Russell 1000 value index,
The top 5 holdings as of 08/31/07

(%) of the Fund's assets

Exxon Mobil	5.19
General Electric	4.80
AT&T	3.32
Citigroup	3.13
BankAmerica	3.04

(VTI) Vanguard Total Stock Market

Category: Large blend

Vanguard has 33 Select Vanguard ETFs from highly targeted sectors to international markets to broad domestic indices. They have significantly lower costs than other ETFs(VTI) seeks to track the performance of a Benchmark Index that measures the investment return of the overall stock market. The fund employs a passive investment management strategy that tracks the performance of the MSCI U.S. broad market index, which consists of all U.S. common stock traded regularly on the NYSE, AMEX, or OTC markets. It typically invest substantially all of its assets in the 1,300 largest stocks in its target index, thus covering nearly 95% of the index's total market capitalization. Generally speaking, (VTI) has an expense ratio of 0.07%. Vanguard ETFs are known to have some of the lowest expense ratios in the industry. The top 5 holdings as of 06/30/07

	(%) of the Fund's assets
Exxon Mobil	2.83
General Electric	2.32
AT&T	1.53
Microsoft	1.53
Citigroup	1.48

(DIA) DIAMONDS Trust

Category: Large Value

DIAMONDS (DIA) are unit investment trusts designed to closely track the price and yield performance of the Dow Jones 30 Industrial Average (DJIA). The trust holds all of the 30 DJIA stocks. DIAMONDS trade on the American Stock exchange.

In 1998, the AMEX listed the DIAMONDS (DIA) Fund. The Dow Jones Industrial Average is the basis for DIAMONDS. The DJIA is the oldest continuous barometer of the U.S. stock market and the most widely quoted indicator of the U.S. stock market activity. The 30 component companies are leaders in their respective industries. The 30 stocks are widely held by small and large individual and institutional investors.

The price of the DIA Index is equal to the price of the Dow Jones Industrials Average divided by 100. For example, when the Dow Jones is equal to 14,000, the DIA will trade at 140. Over the years, changes took place in this list of 30. Some new companies may be added in the future and existing companies may be deleted from the index. Sophisticated investors may wish to compare the price of (DIA) to its Net Asset Value.

The top 5 holdings as of 09/30/07

	(%) of the Fund's assets
I.B.M.	6.89
Boeing	6.14
3M Corp.	5.47
Exxon Mobil	5.41
United Tech.	4.71

(FXI) iShares TRFTSE XINHAU HK China 25

Category: Pacific/Asia ex-Japan Stock

(FXI) operates as a non-diversified investment funds which seeks investment results that correspond generally to the price and yield performance, before fees and expenses, of the XINHAU HK China 25 Index.

The top 5 holdings as of 08/31/07

	(%) of Fund's assets
China Mobil	10.45
Chinas Life Insur.	8.91
Petrochina	7.84
Ind. & Com Banlk	5.84
China Const. Bank	5.82

(DVY) iShares TR Dow Jones Select Dividend

Category: Large Value

(DVY) seeks investment results that correspond generally to the price and yield performance of the Dow Jones select dividends index. The index is comprised of one hundred of the highest dividend yielding securities (excluding REITS) in the Dow Jones U.S. total market index which is a broad based index representative of the total market of U.S equity securities.

The top 5 holdings as of 10/31/07

	(%) of Fund's assets
Altria Group	3.44
First Energy	3.06
FPL	2.93
Merck	2.86
DTE Energy	2.82

(PID) PoweShares International Dividends achievers

(PID) seeks investments results that correspond to the price and yield of an equity index called the broad dividend achievers index. The fund invests in non U.S. common stocks. The stocks are selected on the basis of their consecutive years of dividends growth.

The top 5 holdings as of 09/30/07

	(%) of Fund's assets
NAM-TAI Elect.	5.70
Westpac Bank – ADR	3.09
Tomkins PLC – ADR	2.96
HSBC	2.72
Vodafone	2.72

(IJH) iShares S&P Mid-cap 400

Category: Mid-cap blend

(IJH) seeks investment results that correspond closely to the performance, before fees and expenses, of the S&P mid-cap 400 index. The fund invests at least 90% of its assets in aggregate sample of securities that reflect the predominant characteristics of the S&P mid-cap 400 index. It may hold up to 10% of non-S&P 400 assets including future contracts, options and cash equivalents.

The top 5 holdings as of 09/30/07

	(%) of Fund's assets
Noble Energy	1.01
Lyondell Chemicals	0.98
Expeditor Int'l	0.85
Cameron Int'l	0.84
Jacobs Engineering	0.76

(XLE) Energy Select Sector SPDR

Category: Specialty-Natural Res.

(XLE) investments includes companies from the following industries: oil, gas, energy equipment and services.

The top 5 holdings as of 11/30/07

	(%) of Fund's assets
Exxon Mobil	20.44
Chevron	12.44
Conocophillips	8.70
Schlumberger	5.13
Occidental Pet.	4.27

(IJR) iShares TR S&P Small–cap 600

Category: Small blend

(IJR) seeks investment results that correspond to the performance of publicly traded U.S. small-cap stock securities as represented by the S&P small-cap 600 index. It only holds securities that have been traded for at least six months and that have a price greater than $1 on three or more business days over a twelve month period.

The top 5 holdings as of 09/30/07

	(%) of Fund's assets
Monitowoc	0.96
Crocks	0.94
Shaw group	0.81
Trimble Navigation	0.80

Varian Semiconductor   0.71

(IWN) iShares Russell 2000 Value

Category: Small value.

(IWN) Seeks investment results that correspond to the performance of publicly traded small-cap stocks with the lowest price to book ratios and forecasted growth within the Russell 2000 index, as measured by the Russell 2000 value index.
The top 5 holdings as of 07/31/07

	(%) of Fund's assets
CF Ind.	0.44
Ohio Casualty	0.40
Realty Income	0.36
Emcor group	0.35
Aptar group	0.34

(XLF) SELECT SECTOR SPDR TRX FINANCIAL

Category: Specialty-Financial

XLF investments include companies from the following industries. Banks, diversified financials, insurance and real-estate. The fund will normally invest at least 95% of its total assets in common stock that comprise the relevant select sector index. It seeks to provide investment results that correspond, before fees and expenses, to the price and yield performance of publicly-traded equity securities, of public companies that are components of the S&P 500 and provide financial products and services.
The top 5 holdings as of 11/30/07

	(%) of the Fund's assets
Bank of America	8.47
Citigroup	6.86
JP Morgan Chase	6.39
American Int'l Group	6.17
Goldman Sachs	4.49

(OIH) OIL SERVICE HOLDERS TR

Category: Energy/Specialty-Natural Res.
OIH seeks to diversify investments in the oil service industry.
There are currently 18 companies included in the investment.
Top 5 holdings as of 09/30/07

	(%) of the Fund's assets
Schlumberger	12.35
Transocean	10.83
Baker Hughes	10.21
Halliburton	9.00
Globalsantafe	8.14

(IWB) RUSSELL 1000 I SHARES

Category: Large Blend
(IWB) seeks investment results that correspond to the performance of the 1000 largest U.S. companies in the Russell 3000 Index. as represented by the Russell 1000 index, which measures the performance of the large capitalization sector of the U.S. market..
The top 5 holdings as of 09/30/07

(EWY) iShares MSCI South Korea Index

Category; Pacific/Asia ex Japan
EWY seeks to provide investment results that correspond generally to the price and yield performance of publicly traded securities in the South Korean market as measured by the MSCI South Korea index. The index consists primarily of stocks trading on the
South Korea Stock Exchange.
The top 5 holdings as of 08/31/07

Samsung Electronics	14.26%
Posco	9.53%
Kookmin Bank	5.64%

Shinhan Financial	3.99%
Hyunday Heavy Ind.	3.72%

(ILF) iShares S&P Latin America 40 Index Fund

Category: Latin America.

ILF seeks investment results that correspond closely to the performance before fees and expenses of the S&P Latin America 40 index. It invests in American Depository Receipts, rather than directly holding of companies in Mexico, Brazil, Argentina and Chile.

The top 5 holdings as of 09/30/07

	% of the fund
Cia Vale o Rio Doce – CP ADR	11.67
Cia Vale Do Rio Doce ADR	10.38
America Movil Sab De Cv-ser L	10.37
Petroleo Brazilerio S.A. ADR	8.01
Banco Itau holding Sa – ADR	6.09

(LQD) iShares IBOXX $ INVESTOP INVESTMENT GRADE CROP

Category: Long term Bond

LQD) Seeks investment results that correspond generally to the price and yield performance of the segment of the U.S. Investment grade corporate bond market as defined by the IBOXX $ liquid investment grade Index. The fund typically invests at least 90% of assets in the bonds of the underlying index, and at least 95% of assets in investment grade corporate bonds. The fund may also invest up to 5% of assets in repurchase agreements collateralized by U.S. government obligations and in cash or cash equivalents. It is non-diversified.

The top 50 holdings as of 09/30/07 are:

	% of the fund
Telecom Italia 7.2% 07/18/36	1,06%
Embarq corp. 8% 06/01/36	1.05%

Embarq corp 6.74% 06/01/13   1.04%
Comcast corp. 6.95% 08/15/17   1.03%
Citigroup Inc. 6% 08/15/17   1.03%

(IWV) RUSSELL 3000 iShares

(IWV) seeks investment results that correspond to the performance of the US equity broad market, as represented by the Russell 3000 index
The top 5 holdings as of 08/31/07

	(%) of the Fund
Exxon Mobil	2.94
General Electric	2.43
ATT	1.50
Microsoft	1.43
Citicgroup	1.41

(XLK) SELECT SECTOR SPDR TECHNOLOGY (Amex)

Category: Specialty - technology
(XLK) Seeks to provide investment results that, before expenses, correspond generally to the price and yield performance of publicly traded equity securities of companies that are components of the S&P 500 and make technology products.
The top 5 holdings: as of 08/31/07

	(%) of the Fund
MICROSOFT (MSFT)	9.59%
ATT (T)	7.61%
CISCO (CSCO)	6.61%
IBM (IBM)	5.62%
INTEL (INTC)	5.39%

(XLU) UTILITIES SELECT SECTOR

Category: Specialty- Utilities

(XLU) seeks to replicate the performance, net of expenses, of the Utilities Select Sector Index. The fund invests at least 95% of assets in common stocks that comprise the index. The index includes companies from the electric utilities, multi utilities, independent power producers, energy traders and gas utility industries. The fund is non- diversified.

List of the top ten holdings in (XLU) as of 06/30/07

Stock	Ticker	(%) of the Fund
Exelon	EXC	10.38%
TXU	TXU	6.60%
Dominion Res.	D	6.43%
Southern	SO	5.48%
Duke Energy	DUK	4.90%

(ICF) iShares Cohen & Steers Realty Majors

Category: Specialty-Real Estate

(ICF) operates as a non-diversified investment fund that seeks investment results that correspond generally to the price and yield performance, before fees and expenses, of the Cohen & Steers Realty Majors Index, which consists of selected real estate investment trusts. REITS represent a sector that pays relatively high dividends. (2.91% as of 0/17/07.

It was one of the best performing sectors during the market drop in 2001 and 2002. .

The Top 5 holdings of ICF as of 09/30/07

	% of the fund
Simon Property Group Inc REIT	8.34%
Prologis Trust REIT	7.43%
Vornado Realty Trust	6.87%
Archstone Smith	5.42%
Boston Properties	5.41%

(PPH) Pharmaceutical Holders trust

Category: Specialty-Health

(PPH) seeks to diversify your investments in the pharmaceutical industry. There are currently twenty one companies included in the pharmaceutical HOLDERS.

The largest 5 holdings of the portfolio are:

Johnson and Johnson	21.2%
Pfizer	17.7%
Merck	14.2%
Abbott Lab.	9.5%
Eli Lilly	7.2%

Select Sector SPDR Funds

SPDRs are a family of ETFs that cover virtually every market segment, which means that you can get the kind of investment you want. Select Sector SPDR Funds are unique ETFs that divide the S&P 500 into sector index funds. It is an investment that unbundle the benchmark S&P 500. They give you a possible ownership in a particular sector from a list of nine major industry sectors. Sectors SPDDR have the diversity of a mutual fund, the focus of a sector fund and the tradability of a stock. It gives you the ability to over-weight or under-weight particular sectors to fit your investment goals. The nine sectors are:

Sector	Symbol
Basic Material	XLB
Consumer Staples	XLP
Consumer Discretionary	XLY
Energy	XLE
Financials	XLF
HealthCare	XLV
Industrials	XLI
Technology	XLK
Utilities	XLU

Each of the Select Sector Funds is designed to closely track the price performance and dividend yield of a particular Select Sector index. Each portfolio holds shares of constituent companies included in the S&P 500. The combined companies of all nine Select Sectors represent all the stocks in the S&P 500. You can invest in one or more Select Sectors Fund if it satisfies your specific goals, or if you think that one particular sector within the S&P 500 will outperform the S&P 500 index. When reviewing the above nine sectors at the same time, you can observe how each sector performs relatively to the other sectors.

GOLD RELATED ETFs

Historically gold has been negatively correlated to the U.S. dollar. Gold related ETFs can be bought when you expect the dollar to decline.

(GLD) StreetTRACKS Gold Shares

Category: Precious Metals

(GLD) was launched on November 18, 2004. It gives you an easy access to gold. One share of (GLD) is equal to 1/10 of an ounce of gold bullion It is classified as a grantor trust for U.S. tax purposes.

(GLD) is an active ETF. In 2007 average volume was about 8 million shares a day based on information provided by the world gold council, as of Dec. 2007 (GLD) had 628 metric tons of gold held in vaults in London by HSBC Holding PLC. In comparison the people republic bank of china has 600 metric tons nd the European central banks had 604 metric tons. This is one good example of the popularity of ETFs.

(GDX) Market Vectors Gold Miners ETF

Category: Precious Metals

(GDX) seeks to replicate as closely as possible, before fees and expenses, the price and yield performance of the AMEX Gold Miners Index, a modified market capitalization, weighted index comprised of publicly traded companies involved primarily in mining for gold and silver.

(GDX) and (GLD) The StreetTracks Gold trust shares are ways to play the gold market. It easier to trade these gold related ETFs than to buy the metal outright. You do not have to pay for shipment and storage costs. The shares of (GDX) are more volatile than the shares of (GLD). Mining companies are subject to risks such as costs problems, labor problems and production and operational problems..

The top 5 holdings are as of 05/13/07

Barrick Gold (ABX)	16.42%
Newmont Mining (NEM)	11.93%
Anglogold Ashanti (AU)	7.63%
Gold Corp (GG)	6.58%
GoldField (GFI)	6.23%

FIXED-INCOME ETFs

(See list of Fixed Income ETFs in Chapter 10)

An alternative to open-end mutual funds and individual bonds.

Fixed Income ETFs are an alternative to open-end mutual funds and individual bonds. They give investors another viable choice of investments. Fixed-income ETFs allow investors to purchase a basket of bonds with the ease of buying a stock, while diversifying their fixed-income risk across a large group of bonds. Fixed-income ETFs provide investors with increased visibility to intra-day pricing of baskets of bonds. Fixed-income ETFs are a tool for investors who wish to take a more active approach to manage fixed income securities while maintaining broad diversification. The average expense ratio for fixed income ETFs is about 0.20% which is very low relative to the expense ratio of mutual funds. These ETFs have been designed to provide maximum flexibility and offer several Advantages over individual bonds and bond mutual funds. There is no minimum investment required. The bonds underlying each ETF are very liquid and actively traded. There is daily transparency of bond holdings unlike mutual funds that disclose holdings semiannually. The average expense ratio of fixed income ETFs is relatively low. The bond market has had typically low correlation to the equities, adding fixed income component increases portfolio diversification and reduces volatility. You can use fixed income shares to temporarily park funds while restructuring your portfolio. As part of a sophisticated income investment strategy, you can sell short or buy long fixed-income ETFs. With one trade you are able to attain a level of diversification that would be time consuming and expensive if you bought individual bonds.

How changes in the outlook for interest rates affect fixed-income ETFs allocation

If you expect the general level of interest rates to rise, you may decide to concentrate your investments in the short-range 1–3 years, such as SHY. SHY tracks the price and yield performance of Lehman's 1–3 year Treasury Index. Similarly, if you expect the yield curve to change with short-term rates going up and long-term rates going down, you can buy the 20+ ETF (TLT) and sell short SHY. TLT tracks the price and yield performance of Lehman's 20+ year Treasury index. TRS is the Lehman U.S. Treasury index, which is a market capitalization weighted index, rebalanced monthly, designed to represent public obligations of the U.S. Treasury that have more than one year remaining to maturity. Fixed-income ETFs have a very low total expense ratio (including management fee) of 0.15%. This fee is worth paying in exchange for the diversification offered by the fixed-income ETF in comparison to individual holding of bonds. This cost is in effect an insurance diversification cost. With the uncertainty of owning individual corporate bonds, a diversified ETF reduces part of the risk associated with fixed-income investment. Bond ETFs pay dividends monthly.

Maturity Dates of Fixed-Income ETFs

Fixed-income iShares ETFs never mature. The funds sell fixed-income securities Before maturity dates and reinvest the proceeds and the cash available. The funds attempt To track closely the risks and returns of their respective indices. Fixed income iShares are diversified basket of securities that offer an efficient way to diversify portfolios and gain broad and precise exposure to the fixed income market. Some funds are focused on different maturities of the treasury markets and other funds cover the corporate bonds sector.

(AGG) iShares Lehman Aggregate Bond Fund

Category: Intermediate-Term Bond

On September 23, 2003 Barclays Global Investors launched the iShares Lehman Aggregate Bond Fund (AGG). This fund closely tracks a widely used fixed-income benchmark which is the Lehman U.S. Aggregate Bond Index. It represents taxable investment-grade U.S. dollar-based bond market. These bonds have at least one year until final maturity, and have an outstanding par value of at least $200 million AGG has all the advantages of ETFs such as tax advantage, transparency, liquidity, diversification and a 20-bps expense ratio. It is also important to remember that almost 90% of all pen-end bond funds under performed the Lehman aggregate bond index. Those funds that did perform better than the index did it by taking more risk

To be included in the Lehman Aggregate Bond Index a bond's maturity should be at least one year to final maturity. The quality has to be at least an investment grade.

Liquidity has to be at least 200MM. It has to be US dollar denominated and does not include convertibles, private placements, Strips, CMOs floaters or Eurobonds. ETFs are not only a good alternative to individual bonds, but also an excellent alternative to open-end and closed-end bond funds. Considering the advantages that ETF offer in comparison to open-end funds and taking into account the 20-bps expense ratio (AGG) is an excellent alternative. Instead of incurring the multiple transaction costs associated with the purchase of relatively small lots of individual bond trades, you reduce expenses by purchasing an ETF with a specific maturity range. Small individual investors have difficulty building a small diversified portfolio of individual bonds can invest in fixed-income ETFs. It also reduces the costs associated with the spread between the bid and the ask price. Fixed income ETFs are an important tool in asset allocation decisions because it has negative beta and negative correlation to equities.

(AGG) beta is equal to (-0.06) and the correlation is equal to (-0.52).

(SHY) iShares Lehman 1-3 years Treasury Bond

Category: Short Government

(SHY) is an alternative to cash.

If you have cash in your portfolio (as a result of a sale or an inflow of new money)

You should consider investing in the iShares Lehman 1-3 year fund (SHY). It is also a good alternative to money sitting in a money market fund.

(TIP) iShares Lehman TIPS Bond
(Treasury Inflation Protection)

TIPS are inflation linked bonds. TIP operates as a diversified fund that seeks results that   correspond generally to the price and yield performance, before fees and expenses, of the inflation-protected sector of the U.S. Treasury market as defined by the Lehman Brothers U.S. Treasury inflation Notes Index. TIPS returns have three basic components. The first is a "real" coupon that is set when the bond is issued. The second component is an inflation return that is linked to the U.S. Consumer Price Index. Any change in inflation is reflected in the payment that the TIPS owner receives. The third component is a price return that depends on the price of the bond in the open market which is a reflection of demand for TIPS.

Top Dividend Yielding ETFs

Top dividend yielding ETFs should be considered as candidates for investments. You can overstate, understate or fake earnings (based on acceptable accounting rules) but you can not fake a cash dividend. A dividend paying company by definition is usually profitable. Dividend yielding ETFs are especially attractive during periods of economic slowdown. If you are looking for yield income, dividend paying ETFs could be an alternative to fixed income securities. Dividends could play an important role in your retirement planning. Dividend yields continuously change as prices and the dividend amount change. The following list is based on calculations as of 01/18/2008

Sector/ETF	SYM.	Div. Yield
Vanguard REIT	VNQ	7.35%
KBE Regional Banks	KRE	7.07%
KBW Banks	KBE	6.49%
Claymore/Zacks Yield	CVY	6.21%
First trust Morningstar Dividend Leaders	FDL	5.77%

WisdomTree smallcap d iv.	DES	5.66%
Ameristock 10 Yr. Treas.	GKD	5.49%
WisdomTree High Yield	DHS	5.37%
DJ Wilshire REIT	RWR	5.30%
PowerShares High Yield Dividends	PEY	4.95%
DJ US Real Est.	IYR	4.90%
PowerShares listed prveq	PSP	4.89%
SPDR S&P Div.	SDY	4.56%
BANK Regional HOLDRS	RKH	4.44%
Dow Jones Select div.	DVY	4.29%
Australia	EWA	4.22%
PwrShrs Dyn SmVal.	PWY	4.21%
Lehman 1-3 YR Treas.	SHY	4.21%
Select Sec. Financials	XLF	4.08%
iShares Mangd Lg. Val.	JKF	4.02%
iShares S&P GlbFin	IXG	3.90%
United Kingdom	EWU	3.89%
DJ Regional Banks	IAT	3.76%
Pacific ex Japan	EPP	3.74%
SPDR Int'l Real Est.	RWX	3.61%

WisdomTree ETFs

WisdomTree ETFs are "fundamentally Weighted" in contrast to "market-cap weighted" ETFs. The weighting of WisdomTree ETFs is determined by either the amount of the cash dividends that the companies in each ETF pay or by the dividend yield of the securities in each ETF.

BEAR MARKET ETFs (SHORT ETFS)

(Funds that inversely correlate to benchmark indexes)

An investment in "Short" and "Ultra Short" ETFs is designed to rise in value when stocks fall making it easier for investors to place bearish bets. There are advantages to taking a "long" position in a "short" ETF over directly shorting a security. When you are long an ETF (including a bear Market ETF) your maximum potential loss is only 100% of your investment. But when you are "short" a security there is no limit to the amount you can lose since the security can just keep rising.

For a list of Bear Market ETFs and Bear Market Ultra ETFs go to chapter 10.

(DOG) ProShares Short Dow 30

Category: Bear Market
Seeks daily results that correspond to the inverse (opposite) of the daily performance of the Dow Jones Industrial Average,

(SDS) UltraShort S&P 500 ProShares (AMEX)

Category: Bear Market
Operates as an ETF. It seeks daily investment results that correspond to twice (200%) the inverse (opposite) of the daily performance of the S&P 500 Index. (SDS) has a (-0.99) (minus 0.99) correlation to the S&P 500

(QID) Ultra Short QQQ

Category: Bear Market
Seeks daily investment results before fees and expenses, that correspond to twice (200%) the inverse of the daily performance of the NASDAQ 100 index.

(SBB) Short small-cap 600 ProShares

Category: Bear Market
Seeks daily investment results, before fees and expenses, that correspond to the inverse of the daily performance of the small-cap 600 index.

Read the prospectus and the reports to shareholders. Periodically review your ETFs

Since securities can be eliminated from an index or removed from one sector and placed in another sector, you should periodically review the portfolio components (list of securities in an ETF). Each ETF should be reviewed to make sure that you invest in the ETF that you are actually looking for. There are many ETFs available to investors. The key is making sure that you invest in the ones that are right for you. It is important to remember that new ETFs are continuously being added and old existing funds could be changed or discontinued. ETFs are based on an underlying Index. For that reason, its performance is as bad or as good as the performance of the underlying Index. Before you invest review the ETF's prospectus and the reports to shareholders which includes investment objectives, risks, charges, expenses, top 10 holdings and other information, read and consider them carefully before investing.

There are risks involved in investing, including possible loss of principal.

CHAPTER 10

LIST OF EXCHANGE TRADED FUNDS

Symbol Options   Expense ratio

AEROSPACE & DEFENSE

ITA   DJ U.S. Aerospace & Defense iShares   0.48%
PPA   Y   PowerShares Aerospace & Defense   0.60%

AGRICULTURE

DBA   Y   Agriculture Multi sec. (Comm. Corn, wheat 0.91%
             Soybeans, Sugar)
JJA   ETN iPath Dow J. AIG Agriculture Total Return 0.75%
MOO   Market Vectors ETF TR Agribusness DAXglobal 0.65%

BANKS (REGIONALS

IAT   DJ U.S. Regional banks iShares   0.48%
^JLO   Y   (INDEX) ISE U.S. Regional banks
KRE   Y   KBW Regional ETF   0.35%
RKH   Y   Bank Regional HOLDRS Trust

BANKS (MONEY CENTERS AND REGIONALS)

KBE   Y   KBW Bank Index   0.35%

BANKS (LARGE) AND FINANCIALS

IXG   Y   iShares S&P Global Financials   0.48%
IYG   Y   Dow Jones U.S Financial Services   0.48%
PFI   Y   PowerShares Dynamic Financials   0.63%

| VFH | Y | Financials Vanguard ETFs | 0.25% |
| XLF | Y | Select Sector SPDR TRX Financial | 0.23% |

BASIC MATERIALS

IYM	Y	Basic Materials, iShares trust	0.48%
PRFM		PowerShares Basic Material	0.60%
PYZ	Y	PowerShares Basic Materials	0.60%
VAW	Y	Vanguard Materials ETFs	0.25%
XLB	Y	Basic Materials Sector SPDR	0.23%

BASIC MATERILS (ULTRA-LEVERAGED)

| UYM | Ultra (200%) Basic Materials power | 0.95% |

BASIC MATERIALS ULTRA SHORTS

| SMN | Ultra short Basic Materials | 0.95% |

BIOTECHNOLOGY

BBH	Y	Biotech HOLDRS Trust	
FBT	Y	First trust AMEX Biotechnology	0.60%
IBB	Y	Biotechnology Nasdaq iShares	0.48%
PBE	Y	PowerShares Dynamic Biotech & Genome.	0.60%
^RNDY		(INDEX) ISE Bio-Pharmaceuticals	
XBI	Y	SPDR Biotech StreetTracks	0.35%

BROKER – DEALERS

EXB	Y	Claymore/Clear Global, Brokers & Asset Mgrs	0.95%
IAI	Y	DJ U.S. Broker Dealer iShares	0.48%
KCE	Y	KBW Brokers Asset Mgrs, Trust cust. Banks	0.35%

BUILDING & CONSTRUCTION

ITB		DJ U.S Home Construction iShares	0.48%
PKB	Y	PoweShares Dynamic Building&Constr.	0.60%
^RUF	Y	(INDEX) ISE Homebuilders	

| XHB | Y | SPDR Homebuilders | 0.35% |

BUYBACK

| PKW | Y | Powershares buyback achievers | 0.60% |

COMMODITIES

Powershares Multi Sector Commodity Sector

DBA	Y	Powershares DB Agricultural commodities	0.91%
DBB	Y	Powershares DB Base metals	0.78%
DBE	Y	Powershares DB Energy fund	0.78%
DBO	Y	Powershares DB Oil	0.54%
DBP	Y	Powershares DB Precious metals	0.70%
DBS	Y	Powershares DB Silver	0.54%
DGL	Y	PowerShares DB Gold	0.54%
GLD		StreeTRACKS Gold Shares	0.40%
IAU		iShares Comex Gold Trust	0.40%

COMMODITY Grantor Trust

| DBC | Y | PowerShares Deutsche bk commodity (Grantor trust tax) | 0.83% |
| SLV | | iShares Silver trust, (Grantor trust tax) | 0.50% |

COMMODITY (Limited Partnerships)

| UNG | Y | Natural gas L.P. | 0.60% |
| USO | | United States Oil Limited Partnership | 0.50% |

COMMODITIES iPath, ETNs
(Exchanged Traded Notes)

COW iPath Dow Jones AIG Livestock   0.75%

DJP	iPath D. J. AIG Commodity Total Return ETN	0.75%
EEH	Elements Spectrum Large-cap U.S. ETN	0.75%
GAZ	iPath Dow Jones AIG Natural Gas	0.75%

GSG	Y	iShares GSCI Commodity Indexed trust	0.75%
GSP		iPath GSCI Total Return ETN index	0.75%
JJA		iPath Dow Jones– AIG Agriculture	0.75%
JJC		iPath Dow Jones AIG Copper	0.75%
JJE		iPath Dow Jones AIG Energy	0.75%
JJG		iPath Dow Jones AIG Grains	0.75%
JJM		iPath Dow Jones AIG Industrial Metals	0.75%
JJN		iPath Dow Jones – AIG Nickel	0.75%
OIL		iPath Goldman Sa. Oil Tot. Ret IDX Crude ETN	0.75%

CONSUMER DISCRETIONARY

FXD	Y	First trust consumer discretionary AlphaDEX	0.70%
ITB		iShares Dow Jones US Home construction	
IYC	Y	Consumer Services - Dow Jones iShares	0.48%
PBS	Y	PoerShares Dynamic Media Portfolio	0.68%
PEJ	Y	PowerShares Dynamic Leisure & Entertain.	0.68%
PEZ	Y	Powershares consumer discretionary	0.60%
PMR	Y	PowerShares Dynamic Retail	0.70%
PRFS	Y	Powershares FTSI RAFI consumer services	0.60%
RCD		Rydex S&P Equal weight consumer disc.	0.50%
ROB		Claymore/Robb Report Global Luxury	0.70%
RXI		iShares S&P Global consumer discretionary	0.48%
RTH	Y	Retail Holders	
VCR	Y	Vanguard Consumer Discretionary	0.25%
XHB	Y	SPDR Homebuilers ETF	0.35%
XLY	Y	Consumer Discretion. Select Sec. SPDR	0.23%
XRT	Y	Retail SPDR ETF	0.35%

CONSUMER CYCLICALS GLOBAL

| DPC | | Wisdom Tree Int'l Consumer Cyclical Sector | 0.58% |

CONSUMER ELECTRONICS

| PHW | Y | PowerShare Consumer Electronics | 0.60% |

CONSUMER GOODS ULTRA LEVERAGED

UGE   Ultra consumer goods Proshares (200%)   0.95%

CONSUMER GOODS ULTRA SHORTS (inverse 200%)

SZK   Ultra shorts Consumer goods Proshares.   0.95%

CONSUMER STAPLES

FXG		First trust Consumer Staples Alpha DEX	0.70%
IYK	Y	Consumer Goods Dow Jones iShares	0.48%
KXI		iShares S&P Global Consumer Staples	0.48%
PBJ	Y	PowerShares Dynamic Food & Bever	0.69%.
PRFG	Y	PowerShares FTSI RAFI consumer Goods	0.60%
PRFS	Y	PoerShares RAFI Consumer Service	0.60%
PSL	Y	Poershares dynamic consumer staples	0.60%
RHS		Rydex S&P Equal Weight Consumer Staples	0.50%
VDC	Y	Vanguard Consumer Staples	0.25%
XLP	Y	Consumer Staples-Select Sector SPDR	0.23%

CONSUMER STAPLES GLOBAL

KXI   iShares S&P Global Consumer Staples   0.48%

CONSUMER SERVICES ULTRA LEVERAGED

UCC   Ultra consumer services Proshares (200%) 0.95%

CONSUMER SERVICES ULTRA SHORT inverse 200%

SCC   Ultra Services Consumer Services   0.95%

CURRENCY

DBV	Y	PowerShares DB G10 Currency Harvest fund	0.83%
ERO		Barclay's iPath EUR/USD exch rt	0.40%
FXA	Y	CurrencyShares Australian dollar trust	0.40%

FXB	Y	CurrencyShares British Pound Sterling trust	0.40%
FXC	Y	CurrencyShares Canadian Dollar trust	0.40%
FXE	Y	CurrencyShares Euro Grantor Trust – Rydex	0.40%
FXF	Y	CurrencyShares Swiss Franc trust	0.40%
FXM	Y	CurrencyShares Mexican Peso (opt.. inactive) Div	0.40%
FXS	Y	Currency Shares Swedish Krona trust	0.40%
FXY	Y	Currency shares Japanese yen	0.40%
GBB		Barclay's I path GBP/USD ESCH RT ETN	0.40%
JYN		Barcly's I Path JPY/USD exch. Rt ETN	0.40%
UDN		US Dollar bearish fund	0.55%
UUP		US dollar bullish	0.55%

CURRENCY (CLOSED END)

JGT		Nuveen multi currency short term gov't income	

DEFENSE

PPA	Y	PowerShare Aerospace & Defense	0.68%
^DXS		(INDEX) SPADE defense	
^HSX		(INDEX) Homeland security	

DEFENSIVE

DEF		Claymore/Sabrient Defender (100 stocks) ADRs	0.60%

DIVIDEND-INCOME FOCUSED

CVY	Y	Claymore Zachs yield Hog ETF	0.60%
DVY	Y	Dow Jones Select Dividends iShares	0.40%
FDL	Y	First Trust Morningstar Dividend Leaders	0.45%
FVD		First trust value line dividend Index	0.70%
FXM	Y	Currency Mexico Peso trust	0.40%
LVL		Claymore/BBO high income ETF	0.60%
PEY	Y	PowerShares High Yield Equity Div. achievers	0.50%
PFM	Y	PowerShares Dividends Achievers	0.50%
PHJ	Y	PowerShares High Growth Rate Div. Achievers	0.50%
PID	Y	PoweShares Int'l Div. achievers	0.62%

SDY	Y	Streettracks SPDR Dividends (highest 50)	0.35%
VIG	Y	Vanguard Dividends appreciation ETFs	0.28%
VYM	Y	Vanguard high dividends yield ETF	0.25%

WisdomTree Domestic Equity Dividend Funds

DES		WisdomTree SmallCap Dividend Fund	0.38%
DHS		WisdomTree High-Yield. Equity Fund	0.38%
DLN		WisdomTree Large-cap Dividend Fund	0.28%
DON		WisdomTree MidCap Dividend Fund	0.38%
DTD	Y	WisdomTree Total Dividend Fund	0.28%
DTN	Y	WisomTree Dividend Top 100 Fund	0.38%
EEZ		WisdomTree Earnings top 100 Fund	0.38%
EPS		WisdomTree Large-cap Earnings 500 Fund	0.28%
EXT		WisdomTree Total Earnings	0.28%

WisdomTree International Equity Funds

DBU	WisdomTree International Utilities	0.58%
DEB	WisdomTree Europe Total Dividend Fund	0.48%
DEM	WisdomTree Emerging mkts High Yield equity	0.63%
DEW	WisdomTree Europe High Yielding Equity	0.58%
DFE	WisdomTree Europe SmallCap dividend	0.58%
DFJ	WisdomTree Japan SmallCap dividend	0.58%
DGS	WisdomTree Emerging Mkts Small-cap Div.	0.63%
DIM	WisdomTree International Mid-cap Div.	0.58%
DLS	Wisdom Tree International small-cap div.	0.58%
DND	WisdomTree Pacific ex-Japan Total Div.	0.48%
DNH	WisdomTree Pacif. ex-Japan High-Yield equity	0.58%
DNL	WisdomTree Japan High Yield Equity	0.58%
DOL	WisdomTree International Large-cap Div.	0.48%
DOO	WisdomTree International Div. Top 100	0.58%
DRF	WisdomTree Int'l Financial sector	0.58%
DRW	Int'l real estate	0.58%
DTH	WisdomTree DIEFA High-Yield Equity	0.58%
DWM	WisdomTree DIEFA fund	0.48%

| DXJ | | WisdomTree Japan Total Dividend | 0.48% |

Dividend-Rotation ETF

| IRO | | Claymore/Zacks Dividend Rotation ETF | 0.60% |

Dividends funds (closed-end)

AOD	Alpine Total Dynamic dividend
BDV	Blackrock dividend achievers
DCS	Dreman /Claymore dividends and income
GDV	Gabelli dividend and income
FGF	Sunamerica focused alpha growth
NDD	Neuberger dividend achievers
RPF	Cohen & Steers Premium Income Realty

ENERGY

DBE	Y	PowerShares DB Energy	0.78%
ENY		Claymore/SWM Canadian Energy income	0.65%
FCG	Y	First trust ISE- Revere Natural Gas	0.60%
FXN		Firest trust energy AlphaDEX	0.70%
IGE		Goldman Sachs Natural Resources iShares	0.48%
IEO		DJ Oil & Gas Exploration and Production	0.48%
IEZ		Dow Jones US Oil Equipment & Services	0.48%
IYE	Y	Dow Jones U.S. Energy Sector iShares	0.48%
IXC	Y	S&P Global Energy Sector iShares	0.48%
JJE		iPath Dow Jones – AIG Energy (ETN)	0.75%
OIH	Y	Oil Services Holders	
PRFE	Y	Powershares FTSE RAFI Energy sector	0.60%
PXE	Y	PowerShares Dynam. Energy & Explor.	0.60%
PXI	Y	Powershares dynamic Energy portfolio	0.63%
PXJ	Y	PoweShares Dynamic Oil & Gas, Energy	0.60%
RYE		Rydex S&P Equal weight Energy sector	0.50%
VDE	Y	Vanguard Energy	0.25%
XES	Y	SPDR Oil & Gas Equipment & Services	0.35%
XLE	Y	Energy Select Sector SPDR	0.23%

XOP   Y   SPDR Oil & Gas Exploration & Production   0.35%

Ultra Energy

ENPIX   Profunds Oil&Gas ultra sector mutual funds

ENERGY ALTERNATIVES

GEX   Market vectors global alternative energy   0.65%
NLR   Market Vectors Nuclear Energy   0.65%
PBD   Powershares Global clean energy   0.75%
PBW   Y   PowerShares WilderHill Clean Energy   0.60%
^POW Y   (INDEX) ISE-CCM Alternative Energy
PUW   Y   Powershares wilder-Hill progressive energy 0.60%
PZD   Y   PowerShares Cleantech   0.60%
QCLN   First trust Nasdaq clean energy U.S. liquid 0.60%

ENVIRONMENTAL SERVICES

EVX   Y   Market Vectors Environment services   0.55%

FINANCIALS

EXB   Claymore/Clear Glob. Ex.Brokers, Asset Mgrs 0.65%
FXO   First trust Financial Alpha DEX   0.70%
IAI   Dow Jones US Broker Dealer Index fund   0.48%
IAK   Dow Jones US Insurance Index fund   0.48%
IAT   Dow Jones US regional banks   0.48%
IYF   Y   Dow Jones U.S. Fin. Select Sect SPDR Banks 0.48%
IYG   Y   Dow Jones U.S. Financial Services iShares 0.48%
IXG   Y   Financial - Global S&P iShares   0.48%
KBE   Y   SPDR KBW Bank ETF   0.35%
KCE   Y   SPDR KBW Capital Markets   0.35%
KIE   Y   SPDR KBW Insurance   0.35%
KRE   SPDR KBW Regional banking ETF   0.35%
PFI   Y   Poweshares Dynamic Financial sector   0.60%
PJB   Y   Powershares Dynamic banking Sector   0.63%
PIC   Y   PowerShares Dynamic Insurance portfolio   0.68%

PRFF	Y	Powershares FTSE RAFI Financial sector	0.60%
RKH		Regional banks Holders	
RYF		Rydex equal weight financial	0.50%
VFH	Y	Vanguard Financial	0.25%
XBD	Y	(INDEX) Broker Dealer Sector	
XLF	Y	Select Sec. SPDR Financial (Large Banks)	0.24%

FINANCIALS (ULTRA LEVERAGED)

UYG	Proshares trust ultra financials (200%)	0.95%
FNPIX	Profunds Fin'l Ultra sector (150%)	

FINANCIALS ULTRA SHORTS (inverse 200%)

SKF	Y	Ultra Short Financials ProShares	0.95%

FOOD & BEVERAGE

PBJ	Y	PowerShares Dynamic Food & Beverage	0.60%

GAMING, CASINOS

^SIN	Y	(INDEX) ISE Sindex

GOLD

DGL	Y	Powershare DB gold	0.79%

Gold Grantor Trusts

GLD	StreetTRACKS Gold Trust Gold shares	0.40%
IAU	COMEX Gold trust iShares	0.40%
^HVY Y	(INDEX) ISE Gold	

GOLD & SILVER

GDX	Y	Market Vectors Gold Miners RTF TR	0.55%
		(Van Eck Gold & Silver Mining Stocks)	
^XAU Y		(INDEX) PHLX Gold/Silver	

HEALTH CARE

BBH	Y	Biotech Holders	H
FBT	Y	First trust Amex Biotechnology	
FXH		First trust Healthcare AlphaDEX	0.70%
HHA		Healthshares Autoimune inflammation	0.75%
HHB		Healthshares Patient care services ETF	0.75%
HHD		Healthshares Diagnostics ETF	0.75%
HHE		HealthShares Cardio Devices ETF	0.75%
HHG		Healthshares infectious Disease ETF	0.75%
HHJ	Y	Healthshares Emerging cancer ETF	0.75%
HHK	Y	Healthshares Cancer ETF	0.75%
HHM		Healthshares Metabolic-Endocrine disorders	0.75%
HHN		Healthshares Neuroscience ETF	0.75%
HHP		Healthshares Orthopedic repair ETF	0.75%
HHQ		Healthshares composite ETF	0.75%
HHR		Healthshares Respiratory /Pulminary	0.75%
HHU		HealthShares GI/Gender Health ETF	0.75%
HHV		Healthshares Enabling technologies ETF	0.75%
HHZ		Healthshares Ophthalmology ETF	0.75%
HRD		Healthshares Cardiology ETF	0.75%
HRJ		Healthshares European drugs	0.75%
HRW		Healthshares Dermatology & Woundcare	0.75%
IBB	Y	iShares Nasdaq Biotechnology	0.48%
IHE		ishares Dow Jones U.S. Pharmaceutical	0.48%
IHF		iShares U.S. Healthcare providers	0.48%
IHI		iShares US Medical Devices	0.48%
IXJ	Y	S&P Global Health care iShares	0.48%
		(U.S. 64% Swiss 12.3%, UK 11.2%)	
IYH	Y	Dow Jones Health care Sector iShares	0.48%
JNR		Claymore/Clear Global Vaccine	0.65%
PBE	Y	PoweShares Dynamic Biotech. & Genome	0.64%
PJP	Y	PowerShares Dynamic Pharmaceuticals	0.66%
PPH	Y	Pharmateuticals Holders	
PTH	Y	Poweshares Dynamic Healthcare.	0.60%

PTJ Y   Powershares dynamic Healthcare services 0.60%
PRFH Y   Powershares FTSE RAFI Healthcare sector 0.60%
RYH   Rydex S&P equal weight Health care   0.50%
VHT Y   Vanguard Healthcare ETFs   0.25%
XBI Y   SPDR biotech ETF   0.35%
XLV Y   Select Sector Health care SPDR   0.23%
XPH Y   SPDR Pharmateutical   0.35%

HEALTHCARE (LEVERAGED)

RXL   Ultra Healthcare Proshares (200%)   0.95%
HCPIX   Profunds Healthcare Ultra Mutual fund

HELATHCARE ULTRA SHORT (inverse 200%)

RXD   Ultra short healthcare   0.95%

HOME BUILDERS

ITB   iShares Dow Jones U.S. home construction 0.48%
^RUF Y   (INDEX) ISE Homebuilders
XHB Y   SPDR Homebuilders ETF   0.35%

HOMELAND SECURITY

MYP   Focus shares ISE-CCM Homeland Security

INDUSTRIALS

CGW Y   Claymore S&P Water ETF   0.65%
DIA Y   Dow Jones Industrials DIAMONDS   0.18%
EXI   Global Industrial sector iShares S&P   0.48%
FIW Y   First trust ISE water   0.60%
FXR   First trust Industrials durable AlphaDEX 0.70%
ITA   iShares Dow Jones US Aero space & Defense 0.48%
IYJ   Dow Jones Industrial Sector iShares   0.48%
IYT Y   Dow Jones Transportation avg. iShares   0.48%
PHO Y   Powershares global water Resources   0.67%

PIO		PowerShares Global water	0.75%
PKB	Y	Powershares dynamic building & construc.	0.67%
PPA	Y	PoweShares Aerospace & Defense	0.68%
PRFN		Poweshares FTSE RAFI Industrials	0.60%
PRN	Y	Powershares dynamic Industrials	0.60%
RGI		Rydex S&P equal weight industrials	0.50%
VIS	Y	Vanguard Industrial ETFs	0.25%
XLI	Y	Select Sector Industrials SPDR	0.23%

INDUSTRIALS INTERNATIONAL

DDI	WisdomTree International industrial sector	0.58%
EXI	Global Industrial sector iShares S&P	0.48%

INDUSTRIALS (LEVERAGED)

UXI	Ultra Industrials ProShares	0.95%

INDUSTRIALS ULTRA SHORT (inverse 200%)

SIJ	Ultra Shorts Industrials	0.95%

INDUSTRIALS ("ETF-LIKE" CONGLAMORATE)

GE	Y	GENERAL ELECTRIC

INFORMATION TECHNOLOGY(Also see TECHNOLOGY)

FDN	Y	First trust Dow Jones Internet index fund	0.60%
FXL	Y	First trust Technology AlphaDEX fund	0.70%
HHH	Y	Internet Holders	
IGM	Y	iShares Goldman Sachs technology index	0.48%
IGN	Y	iShares Goldman Sachs Networking	0.48%
IGV	Y	iShares Goldman Sachs Software	0.48%
IGW	Y	iShares Goldman Sachs Semiconductor	0.48%
IYW	Y	iShares Dow Jones US Technology Sector	0.48%
MTK	N	Morgan Stanley Technology	0.50%

NXT	Y	NYSE Arca Tech 100 ETF	0.50%
PHW	Y	PowerShares Dyna. Hardware & Con. Electro.	0.68%
PRFQ	Y	PowerShares FTSE RAFI Telecom & Techno.	0.70%
PSI	Y	PoerShares Dynamic Semiconductors	0.65%
PSJ	Y	PowerShares dynamic Software	0.67%
PTF	Y	PoweShares dynamic Technology portfolio	0.63%
PXN	Y	PowerShares LUX Nanotech	0.73%
PXQ	Y	PowerShares dynamic Networking	0.68%
RYT		Rydex S&p EquAl weight Technology	0.50%
QTEC		First trust Nasdaq 100 Technology	0.60%
SMH	Y	Semiconductors Holders	
SWH	Y	Software Holders	
VGT	Y	Vanguard Infor. Technology	0.25%
XLK	Y	Rechnology Select sectors SPDR	0.24%
XSD	Y	SPDR Semiconductor	0.35%

Information Technology Global

IXN	Y	iShares S&P Global Technology	0.48%

INFRASTRUCTURE

GII	Y	Streettracks Macquarie Global infra.100	0.60%
MIC	Y	Macquarie infrastructure comp. trust	

INFRASTRUCTURE (Closed end funds)

MFD		Macquarie/First Global Infrastr. Util. Div. inc.	3.72%
MGU		Macquarie Global Infrastructure	

INSIDER

NFO	Y	Claymore/Sabrient insider ETF (100) stocks	0.60%

INSURANCE

IAK		DJ U.S. Insurance, Keefe, Barlette & W.	0.48%
KIE	Y	Street tracks KBW Insurance	0.35%

| PIC | Y | PowerShares Dynamic Insurance | 0.60% |

IPO-INITIAL PUBLIC OFFERINGS / SPINOFFS

| CSD | Y | Claymore/Clear spin-off | 0.60% |
| FPX | Y | First trust IPOX – 100 Index fund | 0.60% |

INTERNET

BHH		B2B Internet HOLDRS	
FDN	Y	First trust Dow Jones Internet	0.60%
HHH	Y	Internet HOLDRS Trust	
IAH	Y	Internet Architecture Holders Trust	
IIH		Internet Infrastructure HOLDRS	

LIESURE & ENTERTAINMENT

| PEJ | Y | PowerShares Dynamic Liesure & Ent. | 0.60% |

LUX NANOTECH

| PXN | Y | PowerShares Lux Nanotech | 0.73% |

LUXURY

| ROB | | Claymor/Robb Global Luxury ETF | 0.70% |

MATERIALS (BASIC)

FXZ	Y	First trust Materials AlphaDEX	0.70%
IYM	Y	Dow Jones US Basic Materials Sector	0.48%
MXI		ishares S&P global Materials	0.48%
PRFM		Powershares FTSERAFI Basic Materials	0.70%
PYZ	Y	Powershares ERTF Dynamic basic material	0.63%
RTM		Rydex S&P equal weight materials	0.50%
VAW	Y	Vanguard Materials	0.25%
XLB	Y	Select Sector Materials SPDR	0.24%
XME	Y	SPDR S&P Metals and Mining	0.35%

Materials Basic (Inverse 200% Ultra Short)

SMN   Ultrashort basic materials Proshares   0.95%

MEDIA

PBS   Y   PowerShares Dynamic Media   0.60%

MERGER ARBITRAGE

GDL   Gabelli (closed end)

METALS & MINING

DBB	Y	Powershares Idustrial Metals, Base Met. DB	0.78%
DBP	Y	Precious Metals	0.79%
XME	Y	Streettracks SPDR Meals & Mining	0.35%

NANOTECHNOLOGY

PXN Y   PowerShares Lux Nanotech   0.60%
^TNY Y   (INDEX) ISE-CCM Nanotechnology

NATURAL GAS

FCG Y   First trust ISE Revere Nat.Gas ARX   0.60%
UNG Y   U.S. Natural Gas   0.60%

NATURAL RESOURCES

IGE   Y   Natural Resources iShares Goldman Sachs 0.50%

NEGLECTED STOCKS

STH   Y   Claymore/Sabrient Strealth ETF (150)   0.60%

NETWORKING

IGN   Y   Goldman Sachs IT Networking iShares   0.48%
^NWX   (INDEX) Amex networking
PXQ   Y   PowerShares Dynamic Networking   0.60%

NUCLEAR ENERGY

NLR   Market Vectors ETF TR Nuclear Energy   0.65%

OIL (Commodity)

DBO Y	PowerShares DB Oil	0.79%
DCR	Claymore microshares oil down tradable	1.60%
OIL	iPath Goldman S. Oil Tot Ret. IDX Crude ETN	0.75%
UCR	Claymore micro shares oil up tradable	1.60%
USO	U. S. Oil Fd. L.P., Victoria Bay Asset Mg	0.50%

OIL & GAS (LEVERAGED)

DIG   Ultra Oil & Gas Proshares   0.95%

OIL & GAS ULTRA SHORTS (inverse 200%)

DUG   UltraShort Oil & Gas ProShares   0.95%

OIL & GAS SERVICES & DRILLING

IEO	ishares DowJones US Oil&Gas exploration	0.48%
IEZ	DJ U.S. Oil equipment & Services	0.48%
OIH Y	Oil Service - HOLDRS Trust	
^OOG Y	(INDEX) ISE Oil & Gas Services	
PXJ Y	PowerShares Dynamic Oil & Gas Svc.	0.60%
XES Y	SPDR S&P Oil & Gas Equipment & Ser.	0.35%
XOP Y	SPDR S&P Oil & Gas Exploration	0.35%

PATENT

OTP	Claymor/ocean tomo patent	0.60%
OTR	Claymore/ocean (60) Large-cap	0.60%

PHARMACEUTICALS

IHE	DJ U.S. Pharmaceuticals	0.48%
IHI	iShares U.S. Medical Devices	0.48%

PJP	Y	PowerShares Dynamic Pharmaceutical	0.60%
PPH	Y	Pharmaceutical - HOLDRS Trust	
XLV	Y	SPDR Health care (plus equipment)	0.24%
XPH	Y	SPDR S&P Pharmaceuticals	0.35%

PRECIOUS METALS

DBP	Y	Powershares DB precious metals	0.79%
DBS		PowerShares DB Silver Fund	0.54%
DGL		PowerShares DB Gold fund	0.79%
GLD		StreetTrack Gold Shares	0.40%
IAU		ishares COMEX gold trust	0.40%
SLV		ishares silver trust	0.50%
PMPIX		Profunds precious metals Ultra mutual funds	

PRIVATE EQUITY

PSP	Y	Powershares Listed private equity	0.60%

REAL ESTATE (REIT)

DRW		WisdomTree Int'l Real estate	0.58%
FIO		iShares NAREIT Industrial/office	0.48%
FRI	Y	First trust S&P REIT Index fund	0.50%
FTY		iShares FTSI NAREIT real estate 50 U.S.	0.48%
ICF	Y	Realty iShares Cohen & Steers Majors	0.35%
IIA		ING Clarion Real Estate Income	1.17%
IYR	Y	iShares Dow Jones Real Estate U.S.	0.48%
REM		iShares NAREIT mortgage REIT	0.48%
REZ		iShares NAREIT residential	0.48%
RTL		iShares NAREIT retail	0.48%
RPF		Cohen & Steers Premium income Realty	1.04%
RWR	Y	Street Tracks Real Estate Wilshire	0.25%
VNQ	Y	Vanguard REIT	0.12%

REAL ESTATE (CLOSED- END)

IIA		ING Clarion Real Estate Income Closed-end

NRI	Neuberger Berman Realty income Closed-end
RFI	Cohen & Steers Total Ret.Realty Closed-end
RIT	LMP Real Estate income Closed-end

REAL ESTATE INTERNATIONAL

| DRW | Wisdom tree Intl. real estate fund | 0.58% |
| RWX Y | StreetTracks DJ Wilshire (ex. U.S) Int'l | 0.60% |

REAL ESTATE INT'L (CLOSED-END FUNDS)

IGR	ING Clarion Global Real Estate Income	1.55%
RAP	RMR Asia Pacific Real Estate fund	1.64%
RWF	Worldwide Realty Income fund	1.23%
	Cohen& Steers	

REAL ESTATE GLOBAL FUNDS

IFGL	FTSE EPRA/NAREIT Global Real Estate e-US	0.48%
IFNA	FTSE EPRA/NAREIT North America	0.48%
IFEU	FTSE EPRA/NAREIT Europe	0.48%
IFAS	FTSE EPRA/NAREIT Asia	0.48%

REAL ESTATE (LEVERAGED)

| URE | Ultra Real Estate Proshares (200%) | 0.95% |

REAL ESTATE (SHORT, INVERSE 200%)

| SRS | ProShares Ultra short real estate | 0.95% |

RETAIL

PMR Y	PowerShares Dynamic Retail	0.60%
RTH Y	Retail HOLDRS	
XRT Y	SPDR S&P Retail ETF (85% consumer disc.)	0.35%

ROTATION - SECTOR ROTATION

| PYH Y | Powershares valueline Industry rotation | 0.60% |

| XRO | Y | Claymore/Zachs Sector rotation | 0.60% |

SECURITY HOMELAND

| ^HSX | Y | (INDEX) ISE–CCM Homeland Security | |

SEMICONDUCTORS

^BYT	Y	(INDEX) ISE Semiconductors	
IGW	Y	Goldman Sachs Semiconductors iShares	0.48%
PSI	Y	PowerShares Dynamic Semiconductors	0.60%
SMH	Y	Semiconductor HOLDRS Trust,	H (Active options)
XSD	Y	SPDR Semiconductors	0.35%

SEMICONDUCTORS (LEVERAGED)

| USD | | Ultra Semiconductors Proshares (200%) | 0.95% |

Semiconductors Short (Inverse 200%) Ultra Leveraged

| SSG | | Ultra Shorts Semiconductors | 0.95% |

SILVER (Silver Grantor Trust)

| DBS | Y | Powershares Commodity DB Silver | 0.79% |
| SLV | | iShares Silver trust, Different tax rules | 0.50% |

SOCIALLY RESPONSIBLE

DSI	Y	iShares KLD 400 Social	0.50%
GRN	Y	Claymore/LGA Green ETF	0.60%
KLD		iShares Select Social Index Fund	0.50%
KSF		Claymore/KLD Sudan free large-cap Core	0.50%
PBW	Y	PowerShares WilderHill Clean Energy	0.71%
PZD	Y	Powershares Cleantech portfolio	0.70%

SOFTWARE

| IGV | Y | Goldman Sachs Software iShares | 0.48% |
| PSJ | Y | PowerShares Dynamic software | 0.60% |

SWH	Y	Software HOLDRS Trust	

SPIN-OFF

CSD	Y	Claymore Clear Spin-off	0.60%

STEEL

SLX	Y	Market vector Steel Index ETF	0.55%

TECHNICAL LEADERS

PDP		Powersahres Dorsey,WA Technical leaders	0.60%

TECHNOLOGY

BDH	Y	Broadband HOLDERS	
BHH		B2N Internet Holders	
DBT		Wisdom Tree Int'l Technology	0.58%
FDN	Y	First trust Dow Jones internet	0.60%
FXL	Y	First trust technology AlphaDEX	0.70%
HHH	Y	Interent Holders	
IAH	Y	Internet Architecture Holders	
IGM	Y	Goldman Sachs Technology iShares	0.48%
IGN	Y	Networking Goldman Sachs iShares	0.48%
IGV	Y	Software Index Goldman Sachs iShares	0.48%
IGW	Y	Semiconductors Goldman Sachs iShares	0.48%
IIH		Interent infraxtructure Holders	
IXN	Y	S&P Global Technology	0.48%
IYW	Y	Dow Jones U.S. Technology iShares	0.48%
^MSH	Y	(INDEX) Morgan Stanley high Technology	
MTK	Y	StreetTracks Morgan Stanly High Tech 35	0.50%
NXT	Y	NYSE Arca tech 100 ETF	0.50%
PHW	Y	Powershares Dyn Hardware & Consu. Elec.	0.68%
PSI	Y	PowerShares Dynamic Semiconductors	0.65%
PSJ	Y	PowerShares Dynamic Software	0.67%
PTF	Y	Powershares Dynamic technology	0.60%
PXN	Y	Powershares LUX Nanotech	0.73%

PXQ	Y	PowerShares ETF Dynamic Networking	0.68%
QQQQ	Y	Nasdaq 100	0.20%
QTECY		Nasdaq-100 Technology Sector	0.60%
RYT		Rydex S&P equal weight technology	0.50%
RYTAX		Rydex technology ADV class A	1.86%
RYCHX		Rydex technology class C	2.35%
SMH	Y	Semiconductors Holders	
SWH	Y	Software Holders	
VGT	Y	Vanguard Information Technology ETFs	0.25%
XLK	Y	Technology Select Sector SPDR	0.23%
XSD	Y	SPDR S&P Semiconductor ETF	0.35%

TECHNOLOGY ULTRA (LEVERAGE)

ROM	Ultra technology Proshares (200%)	0.95%

TECHNOLOGY ULTRA SHORT

REW	Ultra short technology	0.95%

TELECOMMUNICATION SERVICES

IXP	Y	S&P Global 200 TelecomSector iShares	0.48%
IYZ	Y	Dow Jones U.S. Telecom iShares	0.48%
PRFQ		Powershares FTSE RAFI Telecom and Tech.	0.60%
PTE	Y	PowerShares Dynamic 30 Telecom&Wireless	0.60%
TBH	Y	Telebras HOLDERS	
TTH	Y	Telecom HOLDRS Trust	
VOX	Y	Vanguard Telecommunication Services	0.25%
WMH		Wireless Holders	
^XTC		(INDEX) North America Telecom	

TRANSPORTATION

IYT	Y	Dow Jones Transport Avg. iShares	0.48%

UTILITIES ELECTRIC

FXU	Y	First trust utilities Alpha DEX	0.70%
GII	Y	Macquarie global infrastructure 100 FTSE	0.60%
IDU	Y	Dow Jones U.S. Utilities iShares	0.48%
PRFU	Y	Powershares FTSE RAFI Utilities	0.60%
PUI	Y	PowerShares Dynamic Utilities	0.60%
RYU		Rydex S&P equal weight Utilities	0.50%
UTH	Y	Utilities - HOLDRS Trust	
VPU	Y	Vanguard Utilities	0.25%
XLU	Y	Select Sector Utilities SPDRS	0.23%

UTILITIES GLOBAL

| DBU | Wisdomtree Global utilities sector fund | 0.58% |
| JXI | iShares S&P global Utilities | 0.48% |

UTILITIES CLOSED-END FUNDS

GLU	Gabelli Global Utility & Income st
MFD	Nacquarie/First Global Infrastruc. Util.
RTU	Cohen & Steers REIT and Uti. income
UTF	Cohen & Steers Select Utility Fund
UTG	Reeves Util. Income fund

UTILITIES (ULTRA-LEVERAGED)

| UPW | Powershares trust ultra (200%) Util. | 0.95% |

UTILITIES ULTRA SHORT (inverse 200%)

| SDP | Proshares ultra short Utilities | 0.95% |

VALUE LINE

| PIV | Y | PowerSahres Value Line Timeliness Selection | 0.60% |
| PYH | Y | PowerShares Value Line industry Rotation | 0.60% |

WATER

| CGW | Y | Claymore S&P Global water Index | 0.65% |

FIW	Y	First trust ISE Water index fund	0.60%
^HHO	Y	(INDEX) ISE-B&S Water	
PHO	Y	Powershares ETF Global Water Resources	0.60%
PIO		Powershares ETF Global Water	0.75%

WIRELESS

PTE	Powershares Dynamic telecom.and wireless	0.67%
WMHY	Wireless - HOLDRS Trust	

MANAGED ETF's

FVL	First trust Valueline 100 ETF	0.70%
PIQ	Powershares Magniquant intellidex top 200	0.63%
PIV Y	PowerShares Valueline Timeliness	0.71%
SFV	SPA Market Grader 40	1.12%
SNB	SPA Market Grader 200	1.12%
SSK	SPA Market Grader Small-cap 100	1.12%
SVD	SPA Market Grader Mid-cap 100	1.12%
SZG	SPA Market Grader Large Cap 100	1.12%
WMW	Elements linked to Morningstar Wide ETN Moat Focus Total Return 20	

EQITY ALLOCATION

FVI	First trust Value Line Equity allocation	0.70%

"ETFs LIKE" COMMON STOCKS

BRKB, GE, XOM

ETFs SEQUENCED BY MAJOR MARKET INDEXES.

Symbol Options

Broad Based Index Funds

S&P500

IVV	Y	S&P 500 iShares Index	0.09%
RPV	Y	Rydex S&P500 Pure Value	0.35%
RSP	Y	Rydex S&P Equal Weight Express Shares	0.40%
SPY	Y	S&P500 SPDR	0.10%
SSO		Ultra S&P500 Proshares	0.95%
IOO	Y	iShares S&P Global 100	0.40%
MKH	N	Market 2000+ HOLDERS	
^NDXY		(INDEX) Nasdaq 100	
^MNX	Y	(INDEX) The Mini Nasdaq-100	
NY	Y	NYSE 100 Index Fund	0.20%
PIV	Y	PowerShares Value Line Timeliness Select .	0.71%
QLD		Ultra QQQ Proshares	0.95%
QQEW	Y	Nasdaq 100 equal weighted, First Trust	0.60%
QQQQ	Y	NASDAQ -100 Index Trust shares	0.20%
^VIX		(INDEX) Volatility	

S&P 500 (Leveraged)

SSO	Proshares Ultra S&P 500 (200%)	0.95%
RYNAX	RYDEX NOVA ADV beta 1.5 S&P500	

S&P 500 (Inverse 200%)

RSW	Rydex S&P 500 (Inverse 200%)	0.70%
SDS	UltraShort S&P 500 ProShares (Inverse 200%)	0.95%

Total Market Funds

AGG		Lehman Aggregate I shares	0.20%
DGT	Y	SPDR Global titans ETF	0.50%
DTD		Wisdom tree total dividend fund	0.28%
EXT		Wisdom tree total earnings fund	0.28%

EZY		WisdomTree low P/E fund	0.38%
FAB		First trust multi-cap value AlphaDex	0.70%
FAD		First trust multi-cap growth alpha DEX	0.70%
FFF	Y	Fortune 500 - Largest 500 by revenue	
FVL		First trust value line 100 Ranked # 1	0.70%
ISI		S&P 1500 iShares	0.20%
IWV	Y	Russell 3000 iShares	0.20%
IWW	Y	Russell 3000 Value iShares	0.25%
IWZ	Y	Russell 3000 Growth iShares	0.25%
IYY	Y	Dow Jones U.S. Total Market iShares	0.20%
IXK	Y	(INDEX) The ISE 50 Index	
IXX	Y	(INDEX) The ISE 100 Index	
IXZ	Y	(INDEX) The ISE 250 Index	
^NYA		(INDEX) NYSE Composite Index	
NYC	Y	NYSE composite Index fund iShares (large blend)	0.25%
ONEQ	Y	Fidelity Nasdaq Composite Tracking stock	0.30%
PGZ	Y	Powershares dynamic aggressive growth	0.65%
PIQ	Y	Powershares dynamic magniquant	0.60%
PIV	Y	PowerShares Value line timeliness Select	0.71%
PRF	Y	Powershares FTSE RAFI 1000	0.60%
PVM	Y	Powershares dynamic deep value	0.65%
PWC	Y	PowerShares Dynamic Mkt, large-cap 49%	0.60%
PWO	Y	PowerShares Dynamic OTC	0.60%
QQEW	Y	First Trust Nasdaq-100 Equal Weight	0.60%
QQXT	Y	First Trust Nasdaq-100 ex-tech	0.60%
TMW	Y	SPDR Total Market	0.20%
VTI	Y	Vanguard Total Stock Market	0.07%
VXF	Y	Vanguard Extended Market (1200)	0.08%

Large-Cap Core Index Funds.

(Companies with over $5 billion in market capitalization)

BST	Y	Claymore/BIR Leaders 50	0.60%
CVY		Claymore Zachs Yield Hog	0.60%
CZG	Y	Claymore/Zachs Growth & Income	0.60%

DDM		Ultra Dow30 ProShares	0.95%
DIA	Y	Dow Jones Industrial Avg. DIAMONDS 30	0.18%
DLN		Wisdom tree large-cap dividend	0.28%
DVY	Y	iShares Dow Jones Select Div.	0.40%
EEH		Elements Spectrum Large-cap U.S. momentum ETN	0.75%
EEZ		Wisdom tree earnings top 100	0.38%
ELR	Y	Streettracks Dow J. Wilshire large-cap core	0.20%
EPS		Wisdom tree earnings 500	0.28%
FEX		First trust large cap core Alpha Dex	0.70%
IVV		S&P 500 iShares Index Fund	0.09%
IWB	Y	Russell 1000 Large-cap	0.15%
JKD		Morningstar Large Core iShares	0.20%
MKH		Large-cap Market 2000+ HOLDRS	
NY	Y	NYSE 100 Large-cap iShares	0.20%
OEF	Y	S&P 100 Large-cap iShares	0.20%
PJF	Y	Powershares Dynamic large-cap.	0.60%
PRF		Powershares FTSE RAFI US1000 largest	0.76%
QQEW		First trust nasdaq 100 equal weighted	0.60%
QQQQ	Y	PowerShares QQQ trust	0.20%
RPV	Y	Rydex S&P500 Pure Value ETF	0.35%
RSP	Y	Rydex S&P Equal Weight Index	0.40%
^RUI	Y	(INDEX) ISE Russell 1000	
SPY	Y	S&P500 SPDR	0.10%
VV	Y	Vanguard Large-cap U.S. Prime Market 750	0.07%
XLG	Y	Rydex Russell top50 US ETF	0.20%
RYNAN		Rydex Nova ADV beta 1.5 S&P 500	
UDPIX		Profunds Ultra Dow30 (leveraged, 200%)	
ULPIX		Profunds Ultra Bull (200% S&P 500)	

S&P500 ETFs

IVV	Y	S&P 500 iShares Index Fund	0.09%
RPV	Y	Rydex S&P500 Pure Value ETF	0.35%
RSP	Y	Rydex S&P Equal Weight Index	0.40%
SPY	Y	S&P500 SPDR	0.10%

Select Sector SPDR

XLB	Y	Material	0.24%
XLE	Y	Energy	0.24%
XLF	Y	Financial	0.24%
XLI	Y	Industrials	0.24%
XLK	Y	Technology	0.24%
XLP	Y	Consumer Staples	0.24%
XLU	Y	Utilities	0.24%
XLV	Y	Healthcare	0.24%
XLY	Y	Consumer Discretionary	0.24%

Large cap (Leveraged)

DDM	Proshares Ultra Dow 30 (200%)	0.95%
SSO	Proshares Ultra S&P500 (200%)	0.95%
QLD	Proshares Ultra QQQ (200%)	0.95%

Large-cap Growth

ELG		SPDR Dow Jones U.S. Large-Cap Growth	0.20%
FTC		First trust large cap growth	0.70%
IVW		S&P 500/BARRA Growth iShares	0.18%
IWF	Y	Russell 1000 Large-cap growth	0.20%
JKE		Morningstar Large-cap growth iShares	0.25%
OTP	Y	Claymore/Ocean Tomo Patent	0.60%
OTR	Y	Claymore/Ocean Tomo Growth (60)	0.60%
PGZ	Y	PowerShares Dynamic Aggressive Growth	0.60%
PWB	Y	PowerShares Dynamic Large-Cap Growth	0.60%
RPG	Y	Rydex S&P500 Pure Value Growth	0.35%
VUG	Y	Vanguard Large-cap Growth VIPERs	0.11%
XGC	Y	Claymore/great co. large cap growth	0.60%

Large-cap Growth (Leveraged)

UKF	Proshares Ultra Russell 1000 Growth (200%)	0.95%

Large-cap growth Shorts Ultra (inverse 200%)

SKK	Proshares Ultra short Russell 2000 growth (200%)	0.95%

Large-cap Value

BMV		Claymore/BIR Leaders Mid-cap Value	0.60%
CLV		Claymore/Robeco Bost. Part. Large-cap value	0.60%
DEF	Y	Claymore/Sabrient Defender	0.60%
DLN		WisdomTree Large-cap Dividend Fund	0.28%
ELV		StreetTracks Dow J. U.S. Large-cap Value	0.20%
FDV	Y	First trust DB Strategic Value Index	0.65%
FTA		First trust large-cap value Alpha DEX	0.70%
IWD	Y	Russell 1000 Value iShares, 1/3 Fin. 1/3 En.	0.20%
IVE	Y	S&P 500/BARRA Value iShares	0.18%
JKF	Y	Morningstar Large Value iShares Index	0.25%
PVM	Y	PowerShares Dynamic Deep Value	0.60%
PWV	Y	PowerShares Dynamic Large-cap Value	0.60%
RFV	Y	Rydex S&P Mid-cap 400 Pure value ETF	0.35%
RPV	Y	Rydex S&P500 Pure value ETF	0.35%
VTV	Y	Vanguard Value VIPERs	0.11%

Large-cap value (Leveraged)

UVG	Proshares Ultra Russell 1000 value	0.95%

Large-cap International

DOL	Wisdom tree Int'l large-cap dividend	0.48%

Large-cap Shorts (Inverse)

DOG	Y	Proshares short Dow 30	0.95%
SH	Y	ProShares Short S&P 500	0.95%

Large cap Ultra Shorts Inverse (Leveraged)

SDS	Proshares Ultra short S&P 500 (200%)	0.95%

Mid-Cap Index Funds

(Companies with market capitalization between $1.5 billion and $10 billion)

Mid-cap Core

CZA		Claymore/Zacks Mid-cap core ETF	0.60%
DON		Wisdom Tree Mid-cap dividend	0.38%
EMM	Y	SPDR D. Jones Wilshire mid-cap	0.25%
EZM		Wisdom Tree Mid-cap earnings	0.38%
FNX		Firs trust mid-cap core Alpha DEX	0.70%
FVI		First trust Value line equity Allocation	0.70%
IJH	Y	Mid-cap S&P 400 iShares	0.20%
IWR	Y	Russell mid-cap index iShares	0.20%
JKG		Morningstar Mid-core index iShares	0.25%
^MID	Y	(INDEX) ISE S&P Mid-cap 400	
MDY	Y	Mid-cap SPDRs, S&P 400 Trust	0.25%
PJG	Y	Poweshares Dynamic Mid-cap Portfolio	0.60%
RFV	Y	Rydex S&P Mid-cap 400 Pure Value	0.35%
VO	Y	Vanguard Mid-cap MSCI US Mid-Cap 450	0.13%
VXF	Y	Vanguard Extended Market VIPERs	0.08%

Mid-cap Ultra (Leveraged)

MVV	Proshares Ultra mid-cap 400	0.95%
UMPIX	Profunds Ultra Mid-cap (mutual fund)	

Mid-Cap Short

MYY	Short Mid-cap S&P 400 ProShares	0.95%

Mid-Cap Ultra Short (Inverse 200%)

MZZ	Proshares Ultra short Mid-cap 400 (200%)	0.95%
RMS	Rydex S&P Mid-cap 400 ETF (Inverse 200%)	0.70%

Mid- Cap Growth

EMG	Y	StreetTRACKS D. J. Wilshire mid-cap growth	0.25%
FVL	Y	First trust Value line 100	0.70%
IJK	Y	S&P Mid-cap 400/ BARRA Growth iShares	0.25%
IWP	Y	Russell mid-cap Growth Index Fund iShares	0.25%
JKH		Morningstar Mid Growth iShares	0.30%

MCG	Y	Claymore/BIR Mid-cap Growth	0.60%
PWJ	Y	PowerShares Dynamic Mid-cap Growth	0.60%
QQXT		First trust Nasdaq 100 ex-Technology sector	0.60%
RFG	Y	RYDEX S&P Mid-cap 400 Pure Growth	0.35%
VOT	Y	Vanguard Mid-cap growth ETF	0.13%

Mid-cap Growth (Leveraged)

UKW	Ultra Russell Mid-cap growth Proshares (200%)	0.95%

Mid-cap Growth Ultra Short

SDK	Ultra Short Russell Mid-cap growth Proshares	0.95%

Mid-cap Value

BMV	Y	Claymore/ BIR Leaders Mid-cap Value	0.60%
EMV	Y	SPDR Dow Jones Wilshire Mid cap value	0.25%
IJJ	Y	iShares Mid-cap 400 BARRA Value	0.20%
IWS	Y	Russell Mid-cap Value iShares	0.25%
JKG		Morningstar Mid Core iShares Index Fund	0.25%
JKI		Morningstar Mid-cap Value iShares	0.30%
RFV	Y	Rydex S&P Mid-cap 400 Pure Value	0.35%
JKI		Morningstar Mid Value iShares Index Fund	0.30%
PWP	Y	PowerShares Dynamic Mid-Cap value	0.60%
VOE	Y	Mid-Cap Value Index ETF	0.13%

Mid-cap value (Leveraged)

UVU	Ultra Russell Mid-cap Value ProShares (200%)	0.95%

Mid-cap Value Ultra Short

SJL	Ultrashort Russell Mid-cap Value ProShares	0.95%

SMALL-CAP Index Funds

(companies with market capitalization of less than $1.5 billion)

Small-cap Core

BES	Y	Claymore/BIR Leaders Small-cap Core	0.60%
DES	Y	Wisdom tree Small-cap Dividend	0.38%
DSC	Y	SPDR Dow Jones Wilshire small-cap Core	0.25%
EES		WisdomTree Small cap Earnings fund	0.38%
FYX		First trust small cap core AlphaDEx	0.70%
IJR	Y	S&P 600 Small-cap Index iShares	0.20%
IWM	Y	Russell 2000 Small-cap Index iShares	0.20%
JKJ		Morningstar Small Core iShares	0.25%
PJM	Y	Powershares dynamic small-cap	0.60%
PRFZ	Y	PoweShares FTSI RAFI 1500 Small-Midsize	0.70%
PZJ	Y	PowerShares Zachs small-cap	0.60%
^RMN	Y	(INDEX) ISE Mini Russell 2000	
^RUT	Y	(INDEX) ISE Russell 2000	
^SML	Y	(INDEX) ISE S&P small-cap 600	
STH	Y	Claymore Sabrient Stealth (2100)	0.60%
VB	Y	Vanguard Small-Cap VIPERs	0.10%

Small-cap Leveraged

SAA	Ultra small cap 600 Proshares (200%)	0.95%
UWM	Ultra Russell 2000 ProShares	0.95%
UAPIX	Profunds ultra small-cap	

Small-cap ultra short (inverse leveraged 200%)

RRZ	Rydex Russell (Inverse 200%)	
SDD	ProShares Small-cap600 Ultrashort, Inverse 200%	0.95%
TWM	ProShares Russell2000 Ultrashort, inverse 200%	0.95%

Small-Cap Growth

DSG	Y	SPDR D. Jones U.S. Small-Cap Growth	0.25%
IJT	Y	S&P Small-cap 600 BARRA Growth iShare	0.25%
IWO	Y	Russell 2000 Growth Index Fund iShares	0.25%
JKK		Morningstar Small Growth Index iShares	0.30%
PBW	Y	PowerShares WilderHill Clean Energy	0.60%
PWT	Y	PowerShares Dynamic Small Cap Growth	0.60%
RZG	Y	Rydex S&P Small-cap600 Pure Growth ETF	0.35%

| VBK | Y | Vanguard Small-Cap Growth VIPERs | 0.12% |

Small cap growth (Leveraged)
| UKK | | Proshares ultra Russell 2000 growth (200%) | 0.95% |

Small-cap Value Funds
DSV		SPDR D. Jones U.S. Small-cap Value	0.25%
IJS	Y	S&P Small-cap 600/BARRA Value iShares	0.25%
IWN	Y	Russell 2000 Value iShares	0.25%
JKL		Morningstar Small Value iShares	0.30%
PWY	Y	PowerShares Dynamic Small-Cap Value	0.60%
RZV	Y	Rydex S&P small-cap 600 Pure Value	0.35%
SCV	Y	Claymore/IndexIQ Small-cap Value ETF	0.60%
VBR	Y	Vanguard Small-Cap Value VIPERs	0.12%

Small-Cap Value (LEVERAGED)
| UVT | | Ultra Russell 2000 Value Prosahres (200%) | 0.95% |

Small-cap Value Shorts (Ultra leveraged inverse 200%)
| SJH | | Ultra Short Russell 2000 value Proshares | 0.95% |

Small-cap Internationals ETFs
DFE		Wisdom Tree Europe small cap dividend	0.58%
DLS		Wisdom tree International small-cap dividend	0.58%
GWX		SPDR S&P Int'l small-cap	0.60%

Small-cap shorts (Inverse)
| RWM | | Shorts Russell 2000 ProShares | 0.95% |
| SBB | | Short small-cap 600 ProShares | 0.95% |

MICRO-CAP Index Funds
FDM	Y	First Trust Dow Jones Select Micro-cap	0.60%
IWC	Y	Russell Microcap Index Fund iShares	0.60%
PZI	Y	Powershares Zacks Microcap	0.60%

Fixed-Income Bonds ETFs

AGG	Y	Lehman iShares aggregate bond	0.20%
BIL	Y	SPDR Lehman 1-3 month T bill ETF	0.13%
BIV	Y	Vanguard intermediate term bond ETF	0.11%
BLV	Y	Vanguard long term bond fund	0.11%
BND	Y	Vanguard total bond market	0.11%
BSV	Y	Vanguard Short-term treasury ETF	0.11%
BWX		SPDR Lehman International Treasury Bond	0.50%
CFT		iShares Lehman credit bond fund	0.20%
CIU		iShares Lehman intermediate/Credit bond fund	0.20%
CSJ		iShares Lehman 1-3 years credit bond fund	0.20%
GBF		iShares Lehman government/credit bond	0.20%
GKA		Ameristock/Ryan 1 year U.S. Treasury	0.15%
GKB		Ameristock/Ryan 2 year U.S. Treasury	0.15%
GKC		Ameristock/Ryan 5 year U.S. Treasury	0.15%
GKD		Ameristock/Ryan 10 year U.S. Treasury	0.15%
GKE		Ameristock/Ryan 20 year U.S. Treasury	0.15%
GVI		iShares Lehman intermediate Gov't/credit bond	0.20%
HYG	Y	iShares iBoxx $ high yield corporate bond	0.50%
IEF	Y	Treasury Bond Fund 7-10 Years iShares Lehman	0.15%
IEI		Lehman 3-7 years Treasury bond	0.15%
IPE	Y	SPDR Barclays capital TIPS ETF	0.18%
ITE	Y	SPDR Lehman intermediate (1-10 yr) Treasury	0.13%
LAG		SPDR Lehman Aggregate Bond (invest. grade)	0.13%
LQD		iShares iBoxx Investment grade corporate Bond	0.15%
MBB	Y	iShares Lehman MBS fixed rate bond	0.25%
PCY		PowerShares Emerging Mkts Sovereign Debt	0.50%
PHB		PowerShares High Yield Corporate bond	
PLW		PowerShares 1-30 laddered Treasury .	
SHV		Lehman short term Treasury bond iShares	0.15%
SHY	Y	Treasury Bond Fund 1-3 Years iShares Lehman	0.15%
TIP	Y	Treasury Inflation Protection (TIPS) iShares	0.20%
TLH		Lehman 10-20 YR Treasury bond	0.15%
TLO	Y	SPDR Lehman Long Term Treasury ETF	0.13%

TLT   Y   Treasury Bond Fund 20+ YR iShares Lehman   0.15%

Municipal Bonds

CXA   SPDR Lehman California Municipal Bond
INY   SPDR Lehman New York Municipal bond
MUB   iShares S&P National Municipal Bonds   0.25%
PVI   PowerShares VRDO Tax Free weekly
PWZ   PowerShares Insured Califor. Municipal Bond
PZA   PowerShares insured Nat'l Municipal Bond
PZT   PowerShares Insured N. Y. Municipal Bond
SHM   SPDR Lehman Short term Municipal bond
TFI   SPDR Lehman Municipal Bonds

Floating Rate Income

EFL   Y   Floating Rates Salomon Brothers Emerging Mkts   1.48%
"Money Market"   Cash in money market is also an ETF

PREFERRED STOCK ETFs

PFF   S&P U.S. preferred stock index iShares   0.48%
PGF   Y   Powershares Financial preferred portfolio   0.60%

OTC Funds

UOPIX   Profunds Ultra OTC (Mutual fund)

OPTIONS WRITING, BUYWRITE FUNDS, COVERED CALLS

Covered calls

BWV   S&P500 BuyWrite ETN Barclays iPath   0.75%
^BXM   Index) CBOE BuyWrite monthly   Index
^BXY   (Index) CBOE BuyWrtie S&P500   Index
           (2% out of the money)
PBP   PowrShares CBOE S&P 500 BuyWrite Portfolio   0.75%

| PQBW | (Index) CBOE NASDAQ-100 BuyWrite | Index |

Covered Calls Closed-end funds

BDJ	BlackRock Enhanced Div. Achiever trust (stocks)	1.18%
BEP	CBOE S&P 500 Covered calls fund	1.06%
BGY	Blackrock International growth and income trust	
BOE	Blackrock Global opportunity Equity trust	1.14%
BWC	BlackRock World investment trust	
EEF	BlackRock enhanced equity Yield fund	1.12%
EOI	Eaton Vance enhanced equity income	1.07%
EOS	Eaton Vance enhanced equity income II	1.08%
ETB	Eaton Vance Tax Managed Buy-Write Income	
ETJ	Eaton Vance Risk Managed diversified equity income	
ETV	Eaton Vance Risk Managed Opportunities	
ETW	Eaton Vance Tax maged Global BuyWrite Opportunities	
EXG	Eaton Vance Tax mged	1.06%
	Global diversified equity income	

BEAR MARKET ETF'S (INVERSE CORRELATION)

DCR	Claymore MACROshares Oil Dn tradable	1.60%
DOG	Short Dow 30 ProShares	0.95%
EFZ	Short MSCI EFAE Proshares	0.95%
EUM	Short MSCI Emerging Markets Proshares	0.95%
MYY	Short MC 400 Proshares	0.95%
PSQ	Short QQQ Proshares	0.95%
RWM	Short Russell 2000 Proshares	0.95%
SBB	Short small-cap600 ProShares	0.95%
SH Y	Short S&P500 ProShares	0.95%

BEAR MARKET ETFS ULTRA (LEVERAGED)

DUG	Ultrashort Oil& Gas Proshares	0.95%
DXD	Ultra short Dow 30 Proshares (200%)	0.95%
EEV	UltraShort Emerging Markets (200%)	0.95%
EFU	Ultrashort MSCI EAFE	0.95%

EWV	Ultrashort MSCI Japan	0.95%
FXP	Proshares Ultra short FTSE/XINHUA China 25	0.95%
MZZ	Ultra short Mid-cap 400 ProShares	0.95%
QID	Ultra short QQQ	0.95%
REW	Ultrashorts Technology ProShares	0.95%
RMS	Ultrashort S&P Mid-cap (2x) Rydex	0.70%
RXD	Ultrashort Healthcare	0.95%
SCC	Ultrashort Consumer Services	0.95%
SDD	Ultrashort smallcap600 Proshares	0.95%
SDK	UltraShorts Russell Midcap growth	0.95%
SDP	UltraShort Utilities ProShares	0.95%
SDS Y	Ultra short S&P500 ProShares	0.95%
SFK	UltrShorts Russell 1000 Growth	0.95%
SIJ	UltraShort Industrials	0.95%
SJF	Ultrashort Russell 1000 Value	0.95%
SJH	UltraShort Russell 2000 value ProShares	0.95%
SJL	Ultrashort Russe;; Mid-cap value	0.95%
SKF	Ultrashort Financials	0.95%
SKK	Ultrashort Russell 2000 growth Proshares	0.95%
SMN	UltraShort Basic Materials Proshares	0.95%
SRS	UltraShort Real estate ProShares	0.95%
SSG	UltraShort Semiconductors ProShares	0.95%
SZK	Ultrashort Consumer goods	0.95%
TWM Y	UltraShort Russell 2000 ProShares	0.95%

BEAR MARKET (MUTUAL FUNDS)

BEARX	Prudent Bear FDd
GRZZX	Leuthold fds asset allocation
URPIX	Profunds Ultra Bear (Inverse double S&P 500)
USPIX	Profunds Ultra short OTC
UWPIX	Profunds Ultra short Dow30

INTERNATIONAL and REGIONAL ETFs

ASIA

Symbol	Options	Name	
ADRAY		Asia 50 ADR BLDRS	0.30%
AIA		iShares S&P ASIA 50	
DND		WisdomTree Pacific ex-Japan total dividend	0.48%
DNH		WisdomTree Pacific Ex-Jap. High Yield Eq.	0.58%
EPP	Y	Pacific Ex-Japan iShares Inc MSCI	0.50%
FNI	Y	First trust ISE Chindia Index fund	
GMF		S&P Emerging Asia Pacific	0.60%
ITF	Y	iShares S&P/TOPIX 150 Index	0.50%
PAF	Y	Powershares FTSE RAFI Asia Pac.ex-Japan	0.80%
PDQ		PowerShares FT.RA.Asia Pa.ex-Jap. Sm.-Mid	0.85%
PUA		Powershares dynamic Asia Pacific	0.80%
VPL	Y	Vanguard Pacific ETF	0.18%
EWM		Malaysia Index Fund iShares MSCI	0.59%
EWS		Singapore Index Fund iShares MSCI	0.59%
EWY	Y	South Korea MSCI	0.74%
EWT	Y	Taiwan Index Fund iShares MSCI	0.74%

ASIA (closed end funds)

IF	Indonesia Fund (closed end fund)	
XXIFX	Indonesia fund (closed end fund)	

AUSTRALIA

EWA	Y	Australia Index fund iShares MSCI	0.54%

CHINA

FXI	Y	China 25 Index iShares Barcley bank	0.74%
GXC	Y	S&P China streettrack SPDR	0.60%
PGJ	Y	PowerShares China USX Golden Dragon Halter	0.60%

China mutual Funds

CHN	China fund (closed-end fund)
MCHFX	Mathews china fund

Hong kong

EWH	Y	iSharesI Hong kong Index fund	0.59%

INDIA

INP	Y	India iPath MSCI ETN	0.89%

JAPAN

DFJ		Wisdomtree Japan small cap Dividend	0.58%
DNL		Wisdomtree Japan high yield equity	0.58%
DXJ		Wisdomtree Japan Total dividend	0.48%
EWJ	Y	Japan Index MSCI iShares	0.59%
ITF	Y	Japan S&P Topix 150	0.50%
JPP	Y	SPDR Russell/Nomura prime Japan	0.50%
JSC	Y	Japan small cap SPDR Russell/ Nomura	0.55%
PJO	Y	Powershares FTSE RAFI Japan	0.75%

JAPAN (ULTRA SHORT)

EWV	ProShares Ultra Short MSCI Japan

JAPAN (closed end)

JEQ	Japan Equity Fund (closed end)
JOF	Japan Smaller cap (closed end)

EUROPE

ADRU	BLDRS Europe 100 ADR	0.30%
CEE	Central Europe and Russia	1.02%
DEB	Wisdom tree Europe total dividend	0.48%
DEW	Wisdom tree Euorope high yield equity	0.58%
DFE	Wisdom tree small-cap. Dividend	0.58%

DTH		WisdomTree DIEFA high yielding equity fund	
DWM		WisdomTree DIEFA fund	
EFA	Y	EAFE, Europe, Austral. & Far East iShares	0.35%
EFG		EAFE Growth Index iShares	0.40%
EFV	Y	EAFE Value	0.40%
EKH		Europe 2001 HOLDRS Depository Rcpt	
EWD		Sweeden	0.54%
EWG	Y	Germany	0.54%
EWI		Italy	0.54%
EWK	Y	Belgium	0.54%
EWL		Switzerland	0.54%
EWN		Netherlands	0.54%
EWO		Austria	0.54%
EWP		Spain	0.54%
EWQ		France	0.54%
EWU	Y	U.K. United Kingdom	0.54%
EZU		European Monetary Union EMU iShares	0.54%
FEU		StreetTracks D. J. STOXX50 (pan Euro.)	0.31%
FEZ	Y	StreetTracks Dow Jones EURO STOXX 50	0.32%
GUR	Y	SPDR S&P Emerging Europe	0.60%
IEV	Y	Europe 350 EUR350 S&P iShares Trust	0.60%
PEF	Y	Powershares FTSE RAFI Europe	0.75%
PEH	Y	Powershares dynamic Europe	0.75%
PWD		PowerShares FTSE RAFI Europe Small-Mid	0.75%
RSX	Y	Russia Market Vectors	0.69%
VEA	Y	Vanguard Euro Pacific ETF, tracking EAFE	0.15%
VGK	Y	Vanguard European Stock ETFs	0.18%

LATIN AMERICA

CH		Chile (closed end fund)	
ECH		iShares MSCI Chile Index	
EWW		Mexico	0.54%
EWZ		Brazil MSCI	0.74%
GML	Y	SPDR S&P Emerging Latin America	0.60%

| ILF | Y | Global iShares S&P Latin America 40 | 0.50% |

MIDDLE EAST & AFRICA

EZA		iShares MSCI South Africa Fund	0.70%
GAF	Y	SPDR S&P Middle east and Africa	0.60%
TKF		Turkey (closed end fund)	

NORTH AMERICA

| ENY | | Claymore/SWM Canadian Energy income | 0.65% |
| EWC | Y | iShares MSCI Canada Index | 0.54% |

RUSSIA

| RSX | Y | Russia ETF | 0.69% |

SOUTH AFRICA

| EZA | Y | iShares MSCI South Africa | 0.74% |

GLOBAL (INTERNATIONAL)

ADRD		BLDRS Developed Markets 100 ADR	0.30%
BIK	Y	SPDR S&P BRIC 40 ETF	0.50%
BKF		iShares MSCI BRIC Index	0.75%
CWI	Y	SPDR MSCI ACWI Global ex U.S.	0.35%
DGT	Y	Global Titans StreetTracks Dow Jones	0.50%
DIM		Wisdom Tree Int'l Mid-cap dividend	0.58%
DLS		Wisdom Tree Intl Small cap Dividend	0.58%
DOL		Wisdom Tree Int'l large cap dividends	0.48%
DOO		WisdomTree International Div. top 100	0.58%
DTH		WisdomTree DIEFA High Yield.Equity	0.58%
DWM		Wisdom Tree DIEFA fund	0.48%
EEB	Y	Claymore/BNY BRIC ETF	
EEN	Y	Claymore/Robeco Developed Int'l Equity	0.65%
EEW	Y	Claymore/Robeco Developed World equity	0.65%
EFA	Y	iShares EAFE,Europe, Austral.&Far East	0.35%

EFG		iShares MSCI EAFE Growth	0.40%
EFV		iShares MSCI EAFE Value	0.40%
EWC	Y	Global i Shares MSCI Canada	0.54%
GMM	Y	Emerging markets ETF	0.60%
GWL		SPDR S&P World Ex-US	0.35%
GWX		SPDR S&P Int'l small cap	0.60%
ILF	Y	Global i Shares S&P Latin America 40	0.50%
IOO	Y	Global iShares S&P 100	0.40%
ITF	Global	iShares S&P TOPIX150 (Tokio)	0.50%
IXC	Y	Global iShares S&P Energy	0.48%
IXJ	Y	Global i Shares S&P Healthcares	0.48%
IXN	Y	Global i Shares S&P Technology	0.48%
IXP	Y	Global i Shares S&P Telecom.	0.48%
PDN		PowerShares Develop Mkt. ex-U.S small-mid	0.75%.
PFA	Y	Powershares Developed Int'l opportunities.	0.75%
PFP		PowerShares Internat'l Listed Private Equity	0.80%
PXF	Y	Powershares FTSI RAFI Developed Mkt ex-US	0.75%
VEU	Y	Vanguard Intern'l all world ex-U.S. Equity	0.25%

EMERGING MARKETS

ADRE	Y	PowerSharesEmerging Markets 50 ADR Index	0.30%
BIK	Y	SPDR S&P BRIC 40 ETF	0.40%
EEB	Y	Claymore/BNY BRIC ETF	0.60%
DEM		WisdomTree Emerging markets high yielding	0.63%
EEM	Y	Emerging Markets MSCI iShares, opt. active	0.75%
FXI	Y	iShares FTSE/Xinhua China 25	0.74%
DGS		WisdomTree Emerging Mkts Small-cap Div.	0.63%
GMF	Y	SPDR S&P Emerging Asia Pacific	0.60%
GMM	Y	SPDR S&P Emerging Markets ETF	0.60%
GUR		SPDR S&P Emerging Europe	0.60%
GXC	Y	SPDR S7P China	0.60%
INP		iPath MSCI India ETN	0.89%
PXH		PowerShares FTSE RAFI Emerging Markets	0.85%
RSX	Y	Russia ETF	0.69%

VWO Y   Vanguard Emerging Markets ETFs Intl equity   0.30%

EMERGING MARKETS ULTRA SHORT
EEV   ProShares Ultra Short Emerging Markets 0.95%

EMERGING MARKETS MUTUAL FUNDS (ULTRA)
UUPIX   Profunds Ultra Emerging Markets

EMERGING MARLKETS MUTUAL FUNDS (ULTRA SHORT)
UVPIX   Profunds Ultra Short Emerging Markets

GLOBAL INT'L BY SECTOR

GLOBAL BROKERS DEALERS & ASSET MANAGERS
EXB   Y   Claymore/Clear Global, Brokers & Asset Mgr. 0.89%

GLOBAL COMMUNICATIONS
DGG   Wisdom Tree Int'l Communications sector   0.58%

GLOBAL CONSUMER CYCLICAL
DPC   Wisdom Tree Int'l Consumer Cyclical   0.58%

GLOBAL CONSUMER NON-CYCLICAL
DPN   WisdomTree Int'l Consumer non-cyclical 0.58%

GLOBAL CONSUMER DISCRETIONARY
RXI   iShares Global Consumer Discret.,45.8% U.S. 0.48%

GLOBAL CONSUMER STAPLES
KXI   iShares Global Consumer Staples, 53.3% U.S.   0.48%

GLOBAL Dividend Focused
DEM   Wisdom tree Emerging Mkts high yield equity 0.63%
DEW   Wisdom tree Europe high yielding equity   0.58%

DGS		WisdomTree Emerging Mkts small-cap Div.	0.63%
DNH		Wisdom tree Pacific ex Japan high yield equity	0.58%
DNL		Wisdom tree Japan high yield equity	0.58%
DOO		Wisdom tree Int'l dividend top 100	0.58%
DTH		Wisdom tree DIEFA high yielding dividend	0.58%
FDD		First Trust DJ STOXX Select dividend 30	0.60%
HGI		Claymore/Zacks International Yield Hog	0.65%
IDV		iShares Dow Jones EPAC Select dividend	0.50%
PID	Y	PowerShares International dividend achievers	0.50%

GLOBAL ENERGY

DKA		Wisdom Tree Int'l Energy Sector	0.58%
IXC	Y	iShares S&P Global Energy (52.2% U.S.)	0.48%
PBD	Y	PowerShares Global Energy	0.75%

GLOBAL ALTERNATIVE ENERGY

GEX	Market vectors Global alternative energy	0.65%

GLOBAL FINANCIALS

DRF		Wisdom Tree Int'l Financial sector	0.58%
IXG	Y	Global iShares S&P Financial (37.3% U.S.)	0.48%
PFI	Y	PowerShares Dynamic Financials	0.63%

GLOBAL FIXED INCOME

BWX	SPDR Lehman International Treasury Bond

GLOBAL HEALTHCARE

DBR		Wisdom Tree Int'l Health Care sector	0.58%
HHT		Healthshares European Medical products	0.95%
HRJ		Healthshares European drugs	0.95%
IXJ	Y	iShares S&P Global Healthcare (64.8% U.S.)	0.48%

GLOBAL INDUSTRIAL

DDI	Wisdom Tree Int'l Industrial Sector	0.58%
EXI	S&P Global Industrials iShares (50.8% U.S.)	0.48%

GLOBAL INFRASTRUCTURE
GII   Y   Streettracks Macquarie Global Infrastruc.100   0.60%

GLOBAL INFRASTRUCTURE (CLOSED-END)
MFD   Macquarie/First Global Infrastr. Utilities income   3.72%

GLOBAL BASIC MATERIAL SECTOR FUND
DBN   Wisdom tree global basic material   0.58%
MXI   ishares S&P global Materials, 20.4% U.S. 0.48%

GLOBAL LUXURY
ROB   Claymor/Robb global luxury ETF   0.70%

GLOBAL MERGER & ACQUISITIONS BUYOUTS
GDL   Gabelli global deal (closed-end)   0.86%

GLOBAL REITS
DRW   Wisdom Tree Int'l Real Estate fund   0.58%
FFR   First Trust Global Real Estate   0.70%
IFGL   iShares EPRA/NAREIT Global Real Estate   0.48%
RWX   Y   SPDR DJ Wilshire INTL Real Estate   0.59%
APFAX   Cohen & Steers Asia Pacific Realty
IRFAX   Cohen & Steers Int'l Realty cl. A

GLOBAL TECHNOLOGY
DBT   Wisdom Tree Int'l Technology sector   0.58%
IXN   Y   iShares S&P Global Technology (69.7% U.S.)   0.48%

GLOBAL TELECOMMUNICATIONS
IXP   iShares Global Telecom. (32.4% U.S.)   0.48%

GLOBAL UTILITIES
DBU   Wisdomtree international Utilities   0.58%
JXI   iShares global Utilities, 35.8% U.S.   0.48%

GLOBAL UTILITIES (CLOSED-END)

GLU   Gabelli Global Utility & Income trust

MFD   Macquarie/First Global Infrastruc. Util. Div.

GLOBSAL WATER

CGW   Claymore S&P Global Water   0.65%

PIO   Powershares Global Water   0.75%

COUNTRY ROTATION

CRO   Claymore/Zachs Country Rotation, 200 0.65%

SHORT INTERNATIONAL ETFs

EEV   ULTRA SHORT MSCI Emerging Markets

EFU   ULTRA SHORT MSCI EAFE ProShares

EFZ   SHORT MSCI EAFE ProShares

EUM   SHORT MSCI Emerging Markets

EWV   ULTRASHORT MSCI Japan

FXP   ULTRASHORT FTSE/Xinhua China 25

CHAPTER 11.

ETFs SPONSOR CONTACT INFORMATION

Ameristock
www.ameristock.com
866-821-6692
Bank of New York – BLDRS
www.bldrsfunds.com
888-627-3837
Barclays ishares
Barclays Global Investors
45 Fremont St.
San Francisco, CA 94105
www.ishares.com
800-474-2737
800-223-5236
Barclay's ipath
www.ipathetn.com
877-764-7284
Claymore Securities
www.claymore.com
866-889-3832
Cohen & Steers
www.cohenandsteers.com
800-330-7348
Deutsche Bank Commodity funds
www.dbcfund.db.com.
877-369-4617

Fidelity-Nasdaq composite
www.nasdaq.com
800-343-3548
First trust Advisors LP
www.ftportfolios.com
800-621-1675
Healthsahres
www.healthsahresinc.com
800-925-2870
HOLDERS (Merrill Lynch)
www.holdrs.com
212-495-1784
iShares
800-474-2737
iShares Distributor and Prospectuses
800-iShares
MACRO shares
www.claymoremacroshares.com
800-345-7999
NYSE Arca
www.nxt100.com
888-798-8324
Powershares Capital Mgt
www.powershares.com
800-983-0903
Profunds
www.Profunds.com
888-776-3637
Proshares
www.proshares.com
866-776-5125
Russell (iShares)
800-474-2737

Rydex currency shares
www.currencyshares.com
800-820-0888
Rydex
www.rydexfunds.com
800-820-0888
State street global (DIA), (SPY)
www.amex.com
800-843-2639
State street
www.ssgafunds.com
866-787-2257
State Street Global Advisors
www.streettracks.com
866-320-4053
StreetTRACKS
225 Franklin Street
Boston, MA 02110
State Street Global Advisors
www.spdrindex.com
877-521-4083
SPDRS (Select Sector)
800-843-2639
See also State Street Global Advisors
866-787-2257
United States Natural gas UNG
www.unitedstatesnaturalgasfund.com
800-920-0259
United States Oil fund USO
www.unitedstatesoilfund.com
800-9200-259
Van Eck Global
www.vaneck.com
888-658-8287

Vanguard
www.vanguard.com
866-499-8473
Vanguard (ETFs) Vipers
www.vanguard vipers.com
Wisdomtree
www.wisdomtree.com
866-909-9473
Prospectuses
Read the prospectuses carefully for the various ETFs products and indexes to better understand the risks involved, the expenses charged and the Fund's objectives..

OTHER SOURCES OF INFORMATION

American Stock Exchange
86 Trinity Place
New York, NY 10006-1872
www.amex.com   www.amextrader.com
212-306-1000   800-843-2639
Bank of New York – BLDRS
www.bldrsfunds.com
1-888-627-3837
Barclays Global Investors iShares
45 Fremont St.
San Francisco, CA 94105
www.iShares.com
1-800-223-5236
Chicago Board Options Exchange
LaSalle at Van Buren
Chicago, IL 60605
"Characteristics and Risks of Standardized Options"
www.CBOE.com
877-THE-CBOE   888-678-4667   888-843-2263

CNBC
www.cnbc.com
Correlation calculations
www.sectorspdr.com
Correlation tracker
Eaton Vance
1-800-836-2414
ETF top ten holdings
www.etfconnect.com
HOLDRS (Merrill Lynch)
www.HOLDRS.com
Index Funds
www.indexfunds.com
iPath ETN
www.iPa.com
1-877-76-iPath
Morningstar
www.morningstar.com
NASDAQ composite
www.nasdaq.com
800-343-3548
New York Stock Exchange
www.nyse.indexes.com
212- 656-3000
Nuveen
www.nuveen.com
800-257-8787
Options Industry Council
www.888options.com
888-OPTIONS
Options Clearing Corp.
440 South LaSalle St.
Chicago, IL 60605
800-537-4258
312-322-6200

Options advisory services
www.optionmonster.com
POWERSharesCapitalManagement
www.powershares.com
630-868-7109
800-983-0903
PROFUNDS
www.Profunds.com
1-888-776-3637
Rating (grades) of ETFs
www.fundgrades.com
Rydex
www.rydexfunds.com
800-820-0888
Securities & Exchange Com.
www.sec.gov
SPDRs (Select Sector)
Amex 1-800-843-2639
www.spdrindex.com
S&P Barra Indexes – Fundamentals
History of P/E, P/Book, Dividends Yield etc.
www.barra.com/research/Fundamentals.aspx
Standard & Poors S&P ETFs
www.spglobal.com
State Street Global Advisors
StreetTRACKS
225 Franklin Street
Boston, MA 02110
www.streettracks.com
1-866-320-4053 or 1-866-787-2257
(for list of fund's holdings)
State Street Global Advisors – SPDRS
877-521-4083
www.spdrindex.com
800-843-2639

Technical Charts
www.barchart.com
Timing Indicators
www.SchaffersResearch.com
Toronto Stock Exchange
www.tsx.com
Treasury FITRs ETF Advisors
www.etfadvisors.com
Vanguard (ETFs) Vipers
www.vanguard vipers.com
www.vanguard.com/visit/vipers
1-866-499-8473
Websites
www.etfbookstore.com
www.etfconnect.com
www.etfguide.com
www.etfmarket.com
www.etfzone.com
www.exchangetradedfunds.com
www.indexfunds.com
ETFs Top Ten Holdings
www.etfconnect.com
Articles, data, and news
Investment News
www.investmentnews.com

The information set forth was obtained from sources which we believe reliable but we do not guarantee its accuracy. Neither the information constitutes a solicitation to buy or sell any securities.

RECOMMENDED READING

Books
Sheldon Natenberg, Options Volatility Trading Strategies, Market Place books Inc., 2007
Bill Johnson, Options Trading 101, From Theory to Application, Morgan James
Publishing, 2007

Russell Wild, Exchange-Traded Funds for Dummies. Wiley Publishing Inc., 2007.
David M. Darst, The ART of Asset Allocation, (Asset Allocation Principles and
Investment Strategies for Any Market). McGraw-Hill, 2003
Taxes and Investing: A Guide for the Individual Investor: www.888options.com

The information set forth was obtained from sources which we believe reliable but we do not guarantee its accuracy. Neither the information constitutes a solicitation to buy or sell any securities.

GLOSSARY

130/30 STRATEGY: A strategy that allows managers to take short positions as well as long positions. This is a short-extension strategy. The strategy is called 130/30 in reference to the proportion of long to short positions.

ABSOLUTE RETURN: A measure of performance often used by Hedge funds. Traditionally Hedge funds set a target rate of return objective, rather than using indices as a benchmark to measure performance. The absolute return performance is not correlated to the overall market direction.

ADMINISTRATOR: A person or an organization responsible of administration of a Hedge fund excluding acting as investment advisor to the fund.

ACCUMULATION PATTERN: A price and volume pattern describing investor absorption of a supply of securities over a period of time. It usually occurs after a decline in the price of a security. Although there is often little change in price during accumulation periods, a favorable uptrend develops once the accumulation is over. One measure of accumulation is On-Balance Cumulative Volume.

ACTIVE MANAGEMENT: An investment approach that seeks to perform better than the average performance of a related market or sector of a market. Active managers depend on research, market forecasts, and their own judgment and experience when making investment decisions.

AGGRESSIVE GROWTH FUND: A mutual fund whose objective is large capital appreciation. It invests in companies with relatively high long-term growth rate. An aggressive fund tends to have a higher degree of risk for investors.

ALPHA: A measure of value added. It indicates a portfolio's manager excess rate of return (risk adjusted) relative to a benchmark. It is a numerical value measuring performance relative to a passive strategy and not related (independent of) to market movements. It yields returns in excess of a simple market portfolio.

ALTERNATIVE INVESTMENTS: usually refers to investments done by Hedge Funds and is often described as a Market-Neutral strategy which is not correlated to market trends. The performance of "alternative investments" does not depend on the performance of the market. "Market" is often defined as the S&P500 or the Russell 3000.

AMERICAN-STYLE OPTION: An option that may be exercised or assigned at any time up to and including expiration day (see also European Option).

AMEX: American Stock Exchange

ANNUALIZED RETURN: The conversion of a return covering a period of less than a year into an annual return.

ANNUALIZED STANDARD DEVIATION: Risk as measured by the variability of performance. A higher risk is a higher standard deviation.

ARBITRAGE: The simultaneous purchase of securities in one market and sale in another to take advantage of a temporary price differential. In an arbitrage, the investor attempts to buy a relatively undervalued security and sell short a relatively overvalued security. On occasion, the buy side can be a stock and the sell side a convertible bond because the stock is selling for less than the value that could be obtained by converting the bond. Profits are achieved when the positions converge and move back to a normal relationship.

ARBITRAGE FIXED INCOME STRATEGY: Takes advantage of pricesinefficiencies between two fixed income securities and at the same time attempts to eliminate interest rates risk If you believe that municipal bonds are undervalued in relations to treasuries, you buy long municipals and sell short treasuries..

ASSET ALLCATION: Refers to the distribution of assets of a portfolio among assets classes (cash, bonds, stocks etc.) Geographic regions (Countries, US, Global etc), Investment strategies (growth, income, small cap, Large cap etc), Investments styles and/or investment advisors

ASSIGNMENT: Notification by the Option Clearing Corporation that an owner of an option exercised their right. For equity and index options, assignments are made on a random basis by the Options Clearing Corp.

AT-THE-MONEY OPTION: When the strike price of an option is equal to the current market price.

AUTHORIZED PARTICIPANT: Institutional investors who are allowed to purchase Creation Units directly from an ETF and redeem Creation Units directly with an ETF. To be an Authorized Participant, an entity must be participant in the Depository Trust Company and must enter into an agreement with the fund's Distributor.

AVERAGING DOWN: Buying additional options or stocks at a lower price than the original purchase to reduce the average cost

BACKING AND FILLING: The action of the market when there is no discernible action, whether up or down. It represents a sideways market and usually takes place during periods of accumulation.

BARRA: A leading software company that separates indexes to growth and value. For example, the S&P500 (SPY) is separated as the S&P500 Value (IVE) and the Ss&P500 Growth (IVW).

BASE PATTERN: A chart pattern that describes an area of consolidation in the price of a stock. A double bottom formation is a base pattern.

BASIS POINT: Equals to 0.01% of yield on fixed income security. For example, if a yield rises from 5.0% to 6.0% the change is equal to 100 basis points

BEARISH: When you think that the market will decline in price

BEAR MARKET: When the general trend of securities prices is down over a period of time. When major market indexes are down more than 20% within six months.

BEAR MARKET RALLY:. A short-term up move in prices within an intermediate downtrend in prices. One of the characteristics of a bear market rally is that prices go up rapidly on relatively light volume.

BEAR OPTION SPREAD: A strategy involving two or more options. You expect to profit from the decline in the price of the underlying security.

BEAR CALL SPREAD: When you buy a call with a higher exercise price and simultaneously sell a call with a lower exercise price. The lower exercise price has a higher premium. It is a credit spread.

BEAR PUT SPREAD: When you sell a put with a lower strike price (lower premium). and simultaneously buy a put with a higher strike price. You hope that the price of the underlying security will decline and the spread will narrow.

BENCHMARK: An index against which a portfolio's performance is measured.

BETA: A statistical measure of stock volatility in relation to market volatility, The S&P500 has a beta coefficient of 1. A beta below 1 indicates that the stock is more stable than the market; a beta above 1 indicates that the stock is more volatile than the market. For example, a beta of 1.2 means that when the market goes up 5%, the stock is expected to go up 6%. If the stock market is down 1%, the stock is expected to be down 1.2%. Beta is computed monthly for all common and preferred stocks.

BID-ASK SPREAD: The difference between the price a buyer is willing to pay and the price the seller is willing to sell.

BLACK-SCHOLES FORMULA: A model for option pricing. It is used to calculate the theoretical value of an option taking into consideration the current price of the underlying stock, option strike price, days left to expiration, expected dividend, expected interest rates, and expected stock volatility.

BLOCK TRADE: A transaction of at least 10,000 shares.

BOOK TO PRICE: Book is the book value for the latest reported year and price is the current market price.

BOX SPREAD: A spread involving four options. A long call and a short put with one strike and a short call and a long put with another strike. For example: Buy June 50 call sell June 55 call and at the same time buy June 55 put and sell June 50 put

BPS: See Basis Points

BREADTH (market): The number of advancing stocks minus the number of declining stocks. When advances exceed declines, breadth is positive. When declines exceed advances, breadth is negative. Market breadth statistics for the week include Issues Traded, Advances, Declines, New Highs, and New Lows.

BREAKOUT (price): When the price of a specific stock breaks away from a trading range; i.e., when it breaks a resistance level on the upside or support level on the downside. An all-time breakout means that the stock is trading a new high (never traded before at this level). Sometimes a breakout also refers to a stock crossing its moving average.

BREAKOUT (volume): Refers to a new high in a series of on-balance volume figures. Such volume breakouts often precede price breakouts; an upside breakout is bullish while a downside breakout is considered bearish.

BULL MARKET: When the general trend of securities prices is up over an extended period of time (six months to one year).

BULL OPTION SPREAD: When an investor buys the lower exercise price and sells the higher exercise price. The spreader hopes that the price of the underlying security will rise. The investor anticipates that the spread will widen.

BULLISH TIME SPREAD: When the investor buys the more distant option and sells the nearby option with the same exercises prices. It is used by investors when the stock is expected to rise.

BUY BACK: The purchase transaction by which you, as the writer of an option, liquidate your position as a writer. Thus, you free yourself from the obligation.

BUY-IN: A situation that occurs when a short seller is forced to cover if no stock can be borrowed to maintain a short position, or when the writer of a naked call has to buy the shares to deliver when the call is exercised.

BUYWRITE: It is a covered call.

CALENDER SPREAD: Also known as horizontal spread or time spread. simultaneous purchase and sale of option contracts in the same underlying stock with the same exercise price but with different expiration dates.

CALL OPTION: An option to buy a security at a specific price (exercise price). The option expires at a specific date (called the expiration date).

CAPITAL GAINS DISTRIBUTION: The distribution is payment to fund shareholders of the net gains realized on securities sold within the fund. The net gain is calculated by subtracting any realized losses from realized gains.

CBOE: Chicago Board of Options Exchange.

CHICAGO BOARD OF OPTIONS EXCHANGE:. It offers investors a continuous auction market where options are bought and sold.

CLOSED-END FUND: A fund with a fixed number of shares that trade on an exchange. A closed-end fund does not issue or redeem shares on a continuous basis. The market price could be below, equal, or above net asset value.

CLOSING OPTION PURCHASE TRANSACTION: You buy an option to close that you previously sold to open. Your reason to closing is to terminate a preexisting option obligation.

CLOSING OPTION SALE TRANSACTION: A transaction performed by the holder of an outstanding option in order to liquidate his position. You sell an option to close that you previously bought to open. You liquidate a preexisting long position.

COLLAR: A spread strategy. You sell a call option and buy a put option with a same expiration. It is used often to hedge a long position in an underlying stock that has a large capital gain. It is a combination of a protective put and covered call writing.

COMMON STOCK: Represents ownership in a corporation. As a shareholder of a common stock, you are entitled to a share in the company's profits. Part of the profits may be paid to you as a dividend.

CONDOR SPREAD: An option strategy that involves four options and four strike prices. It has both limited risk and limited profit potential.

CONDOR SPREAD / LONG CALL: You buy a call at the lowest strike, you write a call at the second strike, you sell a call at the third strike and you buy a call at the highest strike.

CONVERTIBLE ARBITRAGE: An investment strategy generally involving the Purchase of a convertible bond and selling short the underlying common stock

CORE / SATELLITE STRATEGY: An ETF core/ satellite strategy is a combination of "passive" and "active" portfolio management. The Core is an ETFs allocation and active managers are the satellites.

CORRELATION: A measurement of the relationship movements of two variables. A correlation coefficient of (0) (zero) indicates no relationships between the variables. A correlation of (-1) indicates inverse relationship and a correlation of (+1) indicates a perfect 100% relationship. The closer the correlation coefficient is to +1 or -1, the more closely the two variables are related. Correlation statistically measures the strength of the historical relationship between two variables (two securities) returns. When working with correlations never assume that one variable causes a change in another. The square of the correlation coefficient is equal to the percent variation in one variable that is related to the variation in the other. A correlation coefficient of 0.5 means 25% of the variations is related. (0.5 squared = 0.25). A correlation coefficient of 0.7 means 49% of the variance is related (0.7 squared = 0.49).

COVERED CALL: A call is considered covered when you own the securities against which you sold call options.

COVERED PUT, CASH SECURED: When a put is written against cash or short term treasuries so that you can pay for the stock if assigned.

COUPON: In percentage (%) interest payment periodically over the life of the bond.

CREATION UNIT: A large block of ETF shares. Only authorized participants can purchase or redeem shares from an ETF. The creation unit size typically is in multiples of 50,000 shares, but can range from 25,000 to 600,000 shares.

CREDIT SPREAD: When the cash balance in the account increases as the spread is established.

CUBES: Nasdaq 100 Trust (QQQ)

DECAY: See time decay.

DELTA: The rate of change in the theoretical price of an option relative to a change in the price of the underlying security.

DERIVATIVES: A derivative is a financial contract the value of which depends on, or is derived from, the value of an underlying asset such as security or an index. These financial instruments require smaller amount of investments than the underlying assets. They change in value with changes in the value of the underlying assets. Options, futures, warrants, forwards and swaps are known as derivatives. Derivatives are generally more sensitive to changes in interest rates or to sudden fluctuations in market prices and thus a Fund's losses may be greater if it invests on derivatives than if it invests only in conventional securities.

DIAMONDS (DIA): The Dow Jones (30) Industrials Average is the basis for this ETF. Diamonds are designed to closely track the price and yield performance of the DJIA. It is equal to approximately of 1/100 of the DJIA. Thus, if the DJIA is at 9000, DIA is at 90.

DIFFUSION INDEX: Refers to the percentage of stocks above the 10-week moving average.

DISCOUNT (ETF): An ETF is selling at a discount when the market price of an ETF is lower than an ETF's net asset value (N.A.V). In a case of a closed-end fund, when it Is trading at a discount, the market price is below the NAV of the fund.

DISTRIBUTION PATTERN: Describes the process of investor supply overcoming demand during a specific period of time. Distribution is often accompanied by high volatility in price movement followed later by a downtrend.

DIVERGENCE: An index price movement that deviates from the movement of another index. For example, the DJIA may reach new highs, while at the same time, the S&P500 may be declining.

DIVERSIFICATION: A portfolio is considered to be diversified when the underlying securities are in different asset classes, different sectors or different geographic regions. The underlying securities should also have different beta and different correlation.

DIVIDEND INCOME: Payment to ETF shareholders of dividend or interest income earned by the fund.

DOLLAR COST AVERAGING: A disciplined investment strategy that involves making periodic investments (often monthly) of equal mount of money. When the market is down you buy more shares and when the market is up you buy less shares.

DOW JONES INDUSTRIAL AVERAGE (DJIA): An index computed from 30 blue-chip industrial companies. (MMM) 3M Corp., (AA) Alcoa, (MO) Altria, (AXP) American Express, (AIG) American International Group, (SBC) ATT Inc., (BA) Boeing, (CAT) Caterpillar, (C) Citigroup, (KO) Coca Cola, (DD) DuPont, (XOM) Exxon, (GE) General Electric, (GM) General Motors, (HPQ) Hewlett-Packard, (HD) Home Depot, (HON) Honeywell, (INTC) Intel, (IBM) Int'l Business Machines, (JNJ) Johnson & Johnson, (JPM) JP Morgan Chase, (MCD) McDonalds, (MRK) Merck, (MSFT) Microsoft, (PFE) Pfizer, (PG) Procter & Gamble, (UTX) United Technologies, (VZ) Verizon Comm. (WMT) Wall-mart, (DIS) Walt Disney

DOWNTICK: A transaction is on a downtick if it takes place at a lower price than the previous transaction.

DOW THEORY: A theory that defines a major (primary) trend when the DJIA (Dow Jones Industrials Average), the DJTA (Dow Jones Transportation Average), and the DJUA: (Dow Jones Utilities Average) are moving in the same direction -- upward or downward.

DOWNTREND: When the prices of securities are moving in a downward direction over a specific period of time.

EARNINGS PER SHARE LONG-TERM GROWTH RATE: The anticipated annual increase in operating earnings over the next 3 to 5 years.

EBITDA: Earnings Before Interest, Taxes, Depreciation, and Amortization.

EQUAL DOLLAR WEIGHTED INDEX: The number of shares for each stock in the index is determined by buying an equal dollar amount of each stock in the index.

ETFs: Exchange-Traded Funds.

ETNs: Exchange Traded Notes: Unlike ETFs, ETNs are debt instruments. In an ETF, an investor owns a share of an equity index. An ETN tracks an index but is treated as a bond instrument in which an issuer owes the shareholder of the ETN the value of the share at the time. ETNs have credit risk as opposed to equity risk, since there is the possibility the issuer will not be able to pay its debt. ETNs are unsecured obligations of the issuer.

EUROPEAN-STYLE OPTION: An option that can be exercised or assigned only on expiration date (cash settled). In a European option, you cannot have an early assignment. (See also American –style option.)

EVENT- DRIVEN STRATEGY: Takes advantage of investment opportunities created by events such as mergers, shares buy back, spin-offs, bankruptcy reorganization etc.

EXCHANGE-TRADED FUNDS (ETFs): Index tracking funds that trade like stocks on an exchange.

EXCHANGE-TRADED OPTIONS: Call or put options traded on an exchange.

EX-DIVIDEND DATE: An investor who buys a stock on or after the ex-dividend date is not entitled to the dividend. An investor who buys securities before the ex-dividend date is entitled to receive the dividend.

EXPENSE RATIO: Expense ratio of an ETF is the percentage of the fund's average net assets used to pay management fees, administrative fees, etc. An ETF with a lower expense ratio is more attractive to the investor.

EXERCISE PRICE: The price at which the owner of a call or put option can buy or sell the underlying stock.

EXPIRATION DATE: The date on which options expire (cease to exist). American options expire on the Saturday following the third Friday of the expiration month. European options expire on the Thursday of the expiration month.

FIXED INCOME INVESTMENT GRADE CORPORATE BONDS: Are bonds with a rating of at least BBB.

FLOAT: The number of shares available for purchase in the open market. It dose not include the restricted (not registered)shares owned by insiders.

FRONT LOAD: A charge (%) by traditional mutual funds upfront when an investment is made. This charge does not exist in no-load funds or in ETFs.

FUNDAMENTAL ANALYSIS: Examines the underlying value of the company itself, including earnings per share, book value, price per earnings ratio, dividend and yields, statements of assets and liabilities, and profit and losses. Fundamental analysis can apply to one specific company, a sector of a market, an industry, or the market as a whole. It is important for long-term buy-and-hold strategies. It is less important for making day trading decisions.

FUND OF FUNDS: Invest in other funds rather than directly in securities. It enables investors to have access to funds that have high minimum investment requirements.

FUTURES CONTRACTS: Is a contract that provides a buy or a sell of usually commodities, currencies and other financial instruments for a specific price and a specific time in the future.

GAP (PRICE): Each day, the price range of a stock is characterized by its high for the day, its low for the day, and its close for the day. A gap occurs when the price range (high-low for the day) does not overlap the price range for the previous day. It represents discontinuity in the price movement and defines the price change where no shares were traded. Usually the daily trading range overlaps part of the previous daily price range. Identifying gaps is important because gaps often indicate changes in trends. There are several types of gaps: a breakout gap signals the start of a new price move from an accumulation or distribution formation. A down gap occurs when the highest price for a given day is below the lowest price of the previous day. An up gap occurs when the lowest price for a given day is above the highest price of the previous day. Exhaustion gap signals the end of a move. A runaway gap marks the continuation of a move and is often near its halfway point.

GLOBAL MACRO STRATEGY: Using a directional speculation on trends in currencies, interest rates, foreign exchange or stock prices.

GOOD TILL CANCELED ORDER (GTC): A limit order to your broker that remains in effect until it is filled or until you cancel it. In the case of options, the order is canceled when the option expires.

GROWTH STOCK: Stock of a company whose earnings and sales have been growing rapidly and are expected to continue to grow at above-average pace. The stock usually has a low dividend payout to shareholders and a high multiple of earnings per share.

HEDGE: Establishing a new securities position to protect an existing position. For example, if you own a stock (long position), you buy a put option to protect against a market decline.

HEDGE FUND: A limited partnership that uses hedging techniques such as selling short, buying on margin, convertible bonds, call and put options etc. These funds are not regulated by the S. E. C. (but could be regulated in the future). They are primarily sold to wealthy sophisticated investors. Hedge funds managers are generally paid a percentage of profits in addition to regular NAV based management fees. Funds are invested with few restrictions as to investment strategies, leverage and risk exposure.

HEDGE (Variable.): An option strategy that involves writing one covered option and one or more uncovered option.

HIGH YIELD STRATEGY: Investing in debt rated BB or lower. The objective is to earn a relatively high return on invested capital. Evaluating the credit risk involved is critical.

HOLDERS: A type of exchange-traded funds. "HOLDERS" and "Holding Company Depositary Receipts" are service marks of Merrill Lynch & Co., Inc. HOLDERS are securities that represent an investor's ownership in the common stock or ADRs of specified companies of a particular industry, sector, or group of securities. HOLDERS allow investors to own a diversified group of stocks in a single investment that is highly transparent, liquid, and efficient. Holders can only be purchased in 100 round lot share increment.

ILLIQUID INVESTMENTS: Investments that are not readily converted into cash.

IMPLIED VOLATILITY: A measure that calculates expected price swings of an underlying asset and is used as a barometer for option prices. Implied volatility is measured in percentages and referred to an individual underlying stock. "individual volatility" explains current price as opposed to historical volatility. In a theoretical pricing model factors such as strike price, time left to expiration. Underlying stick price, and levels of interest rates can be used to calculate volatility. An increase in implied volatility indicates traders anticipate bigger swings in stock prices.

INCENTIVE FEES: Fees that are based on a percentage performance of a portfolio in addition to management fees based on N.AV.

INDEX: (securities market) measures the price movements of a group of stocks, bonds, commodities, etc. Indexes for specific sectors of the market such as banks, pharmaceuticals and utilities measure the price movement of these sectors.

INDEX FUND: A fund whose portfolio matches that of a specific index (such as the Dow Jones 30 Industrial Average, Standard & Poors 500 etc).

INDEXING: Is the weighting of a portfolio to match the performance of an index(such as the Standard and Poors 500).

INDEX OPTIONS: Calls and puts on indexes of stocks. Listed index options enables investors to use options as a tool in implementing investment strategies. (See chapter on options.)

IN-THE-MONEY OPTION (call option): An option whose exercise price is below the current market price of the underlying stock. For example, when the market price of a stock is 30 and the call option has a strike price of 20, the call option is in-the-money 10 points. If the option is exercised immediately, this 10-point value can be realized.

INTRINSIC VALUE OF AN OPTION: It is the immediate exercise value of an option. It is equal to the market price of the stock minus the striking price of the option. (see also in-the-money)

INVESTMENT ADVISOR: An advisory company that is responsible for ongoing decisions regarding an investment portfolio.

iSHARES: One type of Exchange-Traded Funds. iSHARES is a service mark of Barclays Global Investors.

LARGE-CAP STOCKS: Companies are considered "large cap," or with large capitalization, if they have market value of over $5 billion.

LEAPS: Long-term equity anticipation Securities Options. LEAPS exercise term is longer than equity options. Leaps could expire over three years and up to 39 months. with LEAPS, it is possible to have two expiration dates for the same month. For example, you could have a December 07 and a December 08.

LEAPS (REDUCED VALUE): are used for an Index such as SPX and is equal to (1/10) of the S&P 500 Index

LEVERAGE: The use of a loan to purchase additional securities with the expectation that the price appreciation of the securities plus dividend received will be greater than interest charges.

LIMIT ORDER: An order to your broker to buy or sell at a specific price. The purpose is to avoid buying at an overly price or selling at an excessively low price. You may wish to buy a stock or an option below the current market price. You hopefully will buy when the securities hit your limit order.

LIMITED PARTNERSHIPS: A business entity that has the limited liability of a corporation and the tax advantage of a regular partnership.

LIQUIDITY: A stock is considered liquid when it has the ability to absorb a large increase in trading volume with only a small, insignificant change in price. In a high liquidity situation, the spread between bid and ask is also small.

LONG POSITION: Possession of a stock or an option, either fully paid or on margin. It is held for current income or for future capital gains.

MANAGEMENT INVESTMENT COMPANY: iShares and Sector SPDRs are examples of a Management Investment Company. They track indexes closely, but not every stock in the index has to be purchased.

MARGIN TRANSACTION: Purchase of securities when you invest only part of the capital required and you borrow the remainder using the securities as collateral. The amount of margin requirement (minimum equity) to support the position is regulated by the Federal Reserve.

MARKET CAPITALIZATION: It is the value of the company in the open market. It is calculated by multiplying the price of the stock in the open market times the number of shares outstanding.

MARKET NEUTRAL EQUITY STRATEGY: A trading strategy that attempts to eliminate market risk by combining long and short positions and maintaining a zero beta. Securities are selected in equal dollar amounts for long and short positions. Profits are derived from long positions that are performing well and from short positions that are performing poorly.

MARKET RISK: An investment risk that is related to the overall market rather than to the underlying security.

MARKET TIMING STRATEGY: Involves the establishing of price trends. You Buy when an up trend is being detected and you sell when a down trend is being identified.

MATURITY (AVERAGE): Average maturities of bonds weighted in a portfolio of bonds. The calculation takes into consideration the maturity of each bond weighted by its market value as a percentage of the total value of the portfolio.

MERGER ARBITRAGE STRATEGY (ALSO CALLED RISK ARBITRAGE):An "event driven" strategy of mergers and take-over situations. Long and short positions are taken in the companies involved.

MID-CAP STOCKS: Companies are considered "mid-cap," or middle capitalization, if they have a market value of $1.5 billion to $10 billion.

MODEL (INVESTMENT DECISION RULES): It states the relevant factors to the decision maker. A better model means better performance. An investment management model is a set of specific investment rules.

MOVING AVERAGES: An average covering a specific period of time, such as 200, 50, or days. Typically, in technical analysis, a 200-day moving average is popular because it shows how the market has behaved over the most recent 200-day trading period (about 10 months). In a moving average of prices, you add the latest day price and subtract the oldest day price so that any time, you have the latest 200-day average price. The average is continuously updated.

MSCI: Morgan Stanley Capital International

NAKED OPTION (UNCOVERED): A short call option is uncovered if the seller does not own the underlying stock or is not long another call option. A short put is uncovered if the seller is not long another put or is not short the stock.

NASD: National Association of Securities Dealers

NAV: Net Asset Value per Share is calculated by taking the total assets less liabilities divided by the number of shares outstanding.

(OCC) OPTIONS CLEARING CORPORATION: See Options clearing Corp.

ODD-LOT: A round lot is a lot of 100 shares. Odd lots are fewer than 100 shares.

OPEN-END FUND: A fund in which new shares are created continually on demand. See also closed-end funds.

OPEN INTEREST (OPTIONS): The total number of outstanding option contracts That exist for a specific option (strike price, expiration date, and underlying securities)

OPENING TRANSACTION (OPTIONS): An opening purchase transaction (buy to open) adds long positions to existing total long position. An opening sale transaction (sell to open) adds short position to existing short position.

OPPORTUNISTIC STRATEGY: A variety of investment styles (growth, income, large cap, small cap etc.) is used to allocate assets to achieve superior performance.

OPTION: A contract that gives its owner the right (but not the obligation) to buy or to sell to another investor the underlying security at a specific fixed price (strike price) during a specific period of time (up to expiration date). The option contract also obligates the seller (writer) to deliver the underlying securities if exercised by the owner.

OPTIONS CLEARING CORPORATION (OCC): The issuer and guarantor of all listed option contracts. The OCC is owned proportionally by each of the exchanges trading listed options contracts. The OCC is an intermediary between option buyers and sellers.

OPTION PRICES: The premium the buyer pays to purchase the option and which the seller receives for selling the option.

OPTION WRITER: The seller of an option contract. The seller has the right to Receive a premium and has the obligation to meet the option contract upon assignment by the owner.

OUT-OF-THE MONEY (OPTION): A call option is "out of the money" when The strike price is above the current market price. A put option is "out of the money" When the strike price is below the current price. An "out of the money" option has no intrinsic value. It has only "time" value.

OVERBOUGHT: A stock is considered overbought when its price moves upward too far and too fast. The stock is considered overextended, and a downside price correction is therefore expected.

OVERSOLD: A stock is considered oversold when its price decreases too far and too fast. The stock is considered overextended on the downside, and an upside price reaction is expected.

PAIRS TRADING: Establishing a long position and a short position on two stocks in the same sector creating a hedge position.

PARITY: An option trading at "intrinsic" value with no "time" value.

PASSIVE MANAGEMENT: (Investing) Rather than attempting to outperform an index, passive management of an ETF looks to match the performance (no better or worse) of an index and to achieve this with a low expense ratio.

PERFORMANCE FEE" Is paid to a manager as a percentage of profits rather than as a percentage of assets.

POINT AND FIGURE CHARTS: A method of recording price activity that disregards time intervals and volume. It helps as a tool in determining technical support and resistance levels, price breakouts and in formulating price targets.

PREMIUM (CLOSED-END FUND): An amount paid above the Net Asset value.

PREMIUM (OPTION): The price of an option. It includes both intrinsic value and time value.

PRICE PER BOOK RATIO (P/B ratio): The ratio of the price of the stock in the open market divided by the book value of the company

PRICE PER EARNING RATIO (P/E ratio): Is calculated by dividing the market price of the security by the earning per share. For example: A stock is selling at 50 and the earnings are 2 dollars per share then the P/E is 25. Forecast P/E: Is the current price of the security divided by the consensus forecast of the current fiscal year earnings per share. Trailing P/E is the current price divided by the last 12 months reported earnings.

PRICE WEIGHTED AVERAGE: An average of the market prices of the stocks in an index. In that type of an index, the quantity of each of the stocks is equal.

PROBABILITY: This is the percentage of time an event will occur, if it is repeated many times. For example, if you flip a coin the probability that you will get heads is 50%. A probability of 100% means that there is absolute certainty that the event will take place. A probability of 0% means there is no possibility of the event occurring. In the field of investing, we often deal with probabilities rather than certainties.

PUT OPTION: An option contract giving its owner the right to sell a specific number of shares for a specified price on or before the expiration date.

QUANTITATIVE ANALYSIS: An analysis based on facts and figures rather than on judgment and opinions.

RALLY: A technical term describing an uptrend in prices.

RANDOM MOVES OF STOCK PRICES : A random move of stock prices is a move that cannot be explained. Many academicians claim that stock prices move at random, and therefore came up with the idea of creating the market indexes. If, in fact, stock prices move at random, then there is no added value to active portfolio management.

REBALANCING A PORTFOLIO: Bringing your portfolio back to its original asset allocation mix

REIT: A Real Estate Investment Trust

RELATIVE STRENGTH OF A STOCK: Measured as a ratio of the behavior of a stock price relative to the behavior of another stock, or to a chosen market index over a specified period of time.

RESISTANCE LEVEL: A price range of a stock where it is expected to attract sellers and therefore may stop going up and possibly decline in value. The resistance level is often determined by a moving average, such as the 200-day, or 50-day average. It is also defined as a range where, historically, many shares were previously traded.

RISK-ADJUSTED RETURN: The return a stock has achieved divided by how volatile that return has been over the same time period. An expected return on a stock of 8% and an expected return on a bond of 5% does not take into consideration the relative risk. If the stock has a volatility of 15% and the bond has a volatility or standard deviation of 9%, their risk adjusted return may just be equal.

RISK ARBITRAGE: Involves usually the buying the securities of the company being acquired and the simultaneous selling of securities of the acquiring company. It attempts to take advantage of the pricing discrepancies between the two securities. The risk involved is the probability that the merger may be cancelled or the terms of the deal modified.

RISK (INVESTMENT): The degree of uncertainty in price appreciation and income over a period of time for an investment. In many cases, a higher level of risk means an increase in the probability of investment losses.

RISK/REWARD RATIO: A measure of potential losses relative to potential gains for a specific investment.

ROLLING OVER: Closing an open option position and replacing it with a new opening option position that has the same strike price and usually a later expiration date.

ROUND LOT: 100 shares of a stock.

SEC (Securities and Exchange Commission): A Government Agency that regulates the U.S. financial markets including brokers and Mutual funds.

SECTOR INDEX: An index that measures the performance of a segment of the market, such as small cap stocks, pharmaceuticals, etc.

SECTOR STRATEGY: An investment strategy within a specific sector of the Market such as financials, healthcare, real estate, technology etc,

SELECT SECTOR SPDRS: Designed to represent sectors of the S&P500.

SENTIMENT INDICATORS: A technical term for market indicators that try to measure changes in investors' psychology.

SHARPE RATIO: Is a measure of risk-adjusted return. A higher sharpe ratio has a higher risk-adjusted investment return in comparison to a lower Sharpe ratio. Risk averse investors seek to maximize the value of Sharpe ratio. It is calculated by dividing the excess return (the investment return less the risk-free return) by the investment's standard deviation. It uses standard deviation as a description of risk.

SHORT INTEREST: Represent the total number of shares that have been sold short and remain in a short position (not covered or closed yet) as of a specific date.

SHORT SALE (STOCK): Initiated by borrowing the stock and selling it. You sell a stock that you do not initially own. You profit from the decline in the price of the stock. You cover your short by buying the stock to cover your short.

SMALL-CAP STOCKS: Companies are considered small cap, or with small capitalization, if they have a market value of less than $1.5 billion.

S&P 500 INDEX; An Index consisting of 500 stocks chosen from market size, liquidity and industry group representation. The S&P 500 is designed to be an indicator of U. S. equities and to reflect the risk/return characteristics of the large-cap universe.

SPDR: See SPIDERS

SPIDERS: Standard and Poors Depository receipts, an exchange-traded unit Investment trust based on a composite price index.

SPREAD: A spread involves the buying of one option and selling another option.

SPREAD (HORIZONTAL): Occurs when the two options with the same underlying Stock have different expiration dates but the same strike price.

SPREAD (VERTICAL): Occurs when two options with the same underlying stock have the same expiration date but different exercise prices.

SPY: An ETF that tracks the S&P500. It was the first and still the largest ETF

STANDARD DEVIATION: Measures the variability of returns of an investment portfolio average return. It is a measure of risk. An investment with higher standard deviation is an investment with higher risk. It is the square root of the variance.

STOP ORDERS: An order placed with your broker that becomes a market order when thee stop price is triggered when the price of a stock trades at the stop price. The order could be a day order or a good till cancel order.

STOP LIMIT ORDER: A stop order that becomes a price limit order when the stop is triggered. A limit order is an order to buy or sell at a specific price. It is not a market order.

STRADDLE: A trading strategy consisting of calls and puts of an equal number on the same underlying security with the same expiration date and the same strike price. You can have a long straddle or a short straddle.

STRANGLE: An option position of both out-of-the-money puts and calls with different Strike prices but the same expiration date. In a long strangle both options are owned long, and in a short strangle both options are written (sold short).

STRATEGY: Detailed planning of steps to be taken prior to making a final investment decision.

STREET TRACKS SERIES TRUST: Is an "index fund" consisting of ten separate investment portfolios. State Street Global Advisors (SsgA) manages each fund.

STRIKE PRICE (STRIKING PRICE, EXERCISE PRICE): The price at which the owner of an option can buy in case of a call or sell in case of a put the underlying security.

SUPPORT LEVEL: A price range at which a security is expected to attract buyers. The support level is often determined by moving averages or by identifying a range where a large number of shares have traded over a period of time.

SWAP: The sale of a stock and substitution of it by a purchase of another stock. Tax planning is often a reason to swap stocks, in order to reduce or defer taxes.

TARGET-DATE FUNDS: Funds that are designed to fulfill the need to save for retirement. They typically hold a mix of bonds and stocks and it becomes more conservative as they approach the target retirement date. Also known as Lifecycle funds.

TAX-LOSS HARVESTING: Selling the highest priced shares to create capital loss in order to offset capital gains.

TAX SELLING: The sale of a stock to record a loss for tax purposes. Tax selling often takes place before year-end.

TECHNICIAN: An analyst who studies the historical patterns of price, volume, and Data of a specific stock, sector, or the market as a whole. By contrast, a traditional securities analyst studies the fundamentals of a company such as income statement and balance sheet.

TECHNICAL ANALYSIS: There is a distinction between knowing a company's fundamentals and knowing its stock technically. Technical analysis is the study of historical factors, including price and volume behavior, advancing and declining issues, the level of public optimism and pessimism, and the understanding of investor psychology that affect the demand and supply in the marketplace. Hopefully, these technical tools will help you in predicting future prices and improve the timing of buy, hold, and sell decisions.

TECHNICAL RALLY: This occurs when prices move up after a sharp decline. A technical rally is not expected to be sustained; it is usually short-lived.

TENDER OFFER: An announcement of a bid to acquire some or all of the securities of a corporation.

TERM (INTERMEDIATE, LONG, SHORT): Intermediate term usually refers to a period of less than six months. Long term refers to a period exceeding six months. short term refers to a period of less than three months.

TIME DECAY: The useful life of an option decreases as it gets closer to expiration The speed of the decay increases towards the end of the time left to expiration. It is quantified by theta.

TIME VALUE (OPTION): The price portion of an option that is related to the time left before expiration. The value of an option has two components: the time value and the intrinsic value.

TRACKING ERROR: The amount (%) of an ETF performance that deviates from the benchmark index that it supposed to track. The difference is expected to be small, but an ETF that track less liquid securities will tend to diverge more from the underlying securities

TRADING INDEX (TRIN): A technical timing indicator that is used to identify oversold and overbought market conditions. It is the ratio of advancing issues to declining issues divided by the ratio of volume of advancing issues to the volume of declining issues. A reading of over 1.25 of the 10 days' moving average indicates an oversold market condition. The higher the TRIN the more oversold the market. A reading of below 0.70 for the 10 days' moving average indicates an overbought market condition.

TRAILING P/E The current price divided bt the latest 12 months reported earnings.

TRANSACTION COST: The cost of selling or buying shares including bid-ask spread and or brokerage commissions.

TREND: Represents the direction of a moving average. It is defined as the difference between a current average and a previous average. A primary trend is one that last more than one year. A secondary trend lasts only for a few months.

TREND CHANNEL: The area between two parallel trend lines.

TREND LINE: Connects two or more points on a chart and represents the up slope or down slope of a movement over a period of time.

TRIN: See Trading Index.

TRUST (ETF): A long-term unit investment trust established to accumulate and hold a portfolio of common stocks that comprise an index (such as the Dow Jones Industrial Average for example). The trust is intended to provide investment results that, before expenses, generally corresponds to the price performance and dividend yield of the index.

TRUSTEE (ETF): Usually a bank and trust company (such as State Street Bank and Trust in the case of DIAMONDS).

TWELVE-b1 (12-b1) EXPENSES: A percentage of a fund's assets that is paid for marketing and non-operating expenses usually to brokers. ETFs do not pay 12-b1 expenses.

UNCOVERED CALL WRITING: A short call option sold when the seller does not own the equivalent position of the underlying security.

UNCOVERD PUT OPTION WRITING: A short option position that is not covered by cash in the cash account equal to the amount that has be paid when option is exercised and does not have a corresponding short position in the underlying stock.

UNIT INVESTMENT TRUST: An investment company registered with the SEC, under the investment Company Act of 1940, that purchases a fixed portfolio of securities and then offers units in that trust to investors.

UPTICK: A transaction is said to occur on an uptick when the last sale price is higher than the preceding last sale.

UPTREND: Refers to an upward movement of a series of data over a specific period of time.

VEGA OF AN OPTION: It describes changes in volatility. It is the change in an option value that results from a one unit change in volatility. A vega of 0.10 indicates that a 1 percent change in implied volatility causes a 0.10 change in the value of the option.

VIPER SHARES: Vanguard Index Participating Equity Receipts, which are a class of exchange- traded shares issued by certain Vanguard mutual funds. VIPER shares can be bought and sold continuously throughout the day at market prices.

VOLATILTY: Volatility measures the degree of price fluctuations for an ETF or other securities over a specific period of time (usually a day, a week, or a month). The volatility of the underlying security is an important factor influencing the price (premium) of options. The higher the volatility of the underlying security, the higher will be the premium of its options. A higher volatility means higher fluctuations between the low price and the high price. Volatility is frequently measured in term of standard deviation or beta.

VOLATILITY IMPLIED: See Implied Volatility.

VOLUME, ON BALANCE: A term in technical analysis that measures cumulative volume over a specific period of time and depends on the direction of price movement. It is used as a measure of the amount of money going in or out of a stock. An increase in on-balance volume indicates that the stock is under accumulation.

VRDOs: VRDOs are high quality, floating-rate bonds that provide investors with tax-exempt income in a short-term time frame.

WARRANT: A security entitles its owner to purchase stock at a specific price by expiration date.

WASH SALE RULE: The wash sale rule prevents you from claiming a loss on a sale of stock if you buy replacement stock within the 30 days before or after the sale

WHIPSAW: Occurs when you buy a stock (usually based on technical analysis) for relatively short-term trading and soon thereafter you reversed your decision and sell at a loss.

WRITER (OPTION): The sell of an option that you do not own as an opening transaction(covered or uncovered)

YIELD (CURRENT DIVIDEND): The latest indicated dividend rate that was received as payment to shareholders divided by the latest closing price. The dividend yield indicates the percentage of the latest closing price.

YIELD CURVE: A graph showing the relationship between the time left to maturity (short-term, intermediate-term, and long-term) and the yield at each time left. For example, support you want to know what is the current yield for one year, five years, and twenty-five years. This may help you to determine which maturity and yield combination is more attractive for your portfolio needs.

YIELD TO CALL: Yield on a bond assuming that the bond will be called for redemption on the first call date.

YIELD TO MATURITY: The average rate of return on a bond when held to maturity date. This is a function of time left to maturity, number of interest periods per year, face value, price and interest rate.

YIELD TO WORST: The lowest yield to maturity, yield to call date and yield to put date

ZERO COUPON OBLIGATIONS: Notes and bonds issued at a discount from its face (par) amount. You do not receive any coupon interest payment, monthly, semiannually, or annually, as in the case of a regular bond. You receive the full face value at maturity. the yield to maturity is based on the discount at the time of the purchase.

INDEX

About Nachman Bench Ph.D.

Nachman Bench has more than 25 years of extensive investment experience in Investment Services, Academia, Corporate Business, Quantitative Management, Government, and Publishing. He has been actively engaged in stock and options trading, options income strategies and options hedging for his own personal investments as well as managing portfolios for high net worth individuals and pension funds. He also has extensive professional and academic experience in sophisticated quantitative and statistical technical analysis for stocks sectors and the overall market.

Education
B.S. Mechanical and Industrial Engineering
M.B.A. Finance and Business Administration, New York University
Ph.D. Economics, Quantitative Management, Statistics New York University Graduate School of Business

Awards and Fellowships
Founders Day Award - New York University
Two Ford Foundation Fellowships

Government Appointments
Consultant and Acting Deputy City Administrator of New York City

Established a management science unit for the city government. Designed a computerized information system for the Department of Welfare.

Lectured on Supply Side Economics for the International Communication Agency of the U.S. Government.

Investment Experience

Founder and President of Bench Securities Corp.

An (NASD) National Association of Securities Dealers member

Clearing transactions with Bear Stearns and Morgan Stanley

President of Bench Asset Management, an SEC registered portfolio management firm

Publisher and Editor of the Bench Investment Letter.

Vice President Alex Brown - Deutche Bank, portfolio management for private clients

Consultant to AETNA. Developed computer simulation models for common stock investments.

Consultant to Merrill Lynch. Developed computer models for the stock market timing.

Teaching Experience

Full Professor of Business Management - City University of New York

Dr. Bench has also taught courses at Adelphi University, The New School of Social Research, and the Polytechnic Institute of Brooklyn New York.

Public Companies

Founder, President, and majority shareholder of Special Studies Inc, an information systems consulting and training firm.

Founder, President, and majority shareholder of Funds Management Systems and Bench Group Inc., a money management firm.

Published Books

Questions and Answers about Today's Securities Market (1987). Prentice Hall

The Smart Investor's Guide for Investing - Sectors, Index trading and ETF's (Exchange Traded Funds) (2003). 1st Books Library

Dr. Bench also has written and presented many professional papers including "The Separation of Non-Random Moves from Random Moves in Stock Market Behavior

A resident of Tenafly, NJ, since 1970, Dr. Bench is married and the father of two children.

Email Address

benchn@optonline.net

Printed in the United States
202711BV00002B/172-183/P

9 781434 373144